Dramascr

Great
Escapes

Orpheus and Eurydice

Mr Mukherjee,
Ghostcatcher

Anansi and the Moon

The Casket of Huemac

Four traditional tales dramatised by
ADRIAN FLYNN
with explanatory notes and activities

Nelson

Nelson
Nelson House
Mayfield Road
Walton-on-Thames
Surrey KT12 5PL
United Kingdom

Project management by Elizabeth Paren
Designed and formatted by Geoffrey Wadsley
Art editing by Jane Taylor
Cover illustration by Dave Grimwood, Pelican Graphics
Black and white illustrations by Chris Price and Gerry Grace *(Casket of Huemac)*
Printed by L. Rex Printing Co. Ltd, China

This edition first published by Nelson 2000
ISBN 0-17-432613-0
9 8 7 6 5 4 3 2 1
03   02   01   00

CONTENTS

SERIES EDITOR'S INTRODUCTION

Dramascripts is an exciting series of plays especially chosen for students in the lower and middle years of secondary school. The titles range from the best in modern writing to adaptations of classic texts such as *A Christmas Carol* and *Silas Marner*.

Dramascripts can be read or acted purely for the enjoyment and stimulation that they provide; however, each play in the series also offers all the support that pupils need in working with the text in the classroom:

- **Introduction** – this offers important background information and explains something about the ways in which the play came to be written.
- **Script** – this is clearly set out in ways that make the play easy to handle in the classroom.
- **Notes** explain references that pupils might not understand, and language points that are not obvious.
- **Activities** – at the end of scenes, acts or sections – give pupils the opportunity to explore the play more fully. Types of activity include: discussion, writing, hot-seating, improvisation, acting, freeze-framing, story-boarding and artwork.
- **Looking Back at the Play** – this section has further activities for more extended work on the play as a whole, with emphasis on characters, plots, themes and language.

John O'Connor

WORLDWIDE DRAMASCRIPTS

Whether we look at the Caribbean or China, ancient India or medieval Europe, we find that cultures across the world and throughout history have had one fundamental thing in common: they have all created myths, legends and traditional tales, in an endeavour to make sense of their existence and to confront the most challenging issues of right and wrong.

Worldwide Dramascripts present some of the most exciting and intriguing examples of these tales in the form of lively and thought-provoking playscripts. These bring together figures such as Theseus and Rama, Anansi and Guinevere, Hanuman the monkey-god and the famous Lambton Worm.

With the exception of *Goat Song* – an original retelling of Greek myths in a single play – each anthology brings together three or four short plays with a connecting theme, raising questions about:

- right and wrong
- justice and retribution
- the nature of heroism
- the eternal tensions between brothers and sisters
- the joys and pain of love
- the never-ending need to escape.

Because they feature such basic human concerns the plays and activities in Worldwide Dramascripts offer opportunities for students to engage with issues of enduring significance while enjoying some of the greatest stories ever told.

John O'Connor

V

INTRODUCTION

Sometimes people need to escape.

The plays in this anthology are based on four traditional stories, widely separated in time and country of origin, but all connected by the idea of getting away from unhappy or dangerous circumstances. The ancient Greek story of *Orpheus and Eurydice*, reworked to draw out a contemporary theme, deals with an attempt to escape from death itself. The chilling Aztec tale of *The Casket of Huemac* looks at a desperate attempt to break free from poverty and at the terrible price that may be paid in doing so (only to be read by those with nerves of steel). The Bengali story, *Mr Mukherjee, Ghostcatcher* and the West African tale of *Anansi and the Moon* are more comic views of escape. The former suggests that a quarrelsome home can be something we want to get away from, while the latter deals with an unusual physical danger. Perhaps it is only fair to warn readers that not all the attempts at escape are successful.

  The plays are intended to be read or performed in small groups. Occasionally an extra character has been added to the original story to make it easier to dramatise. Some suggestions for music, sets and lighting are given, but there is plenty of scope for readers to use their own imaginations in staging the plays. As with any play, the text is just a starting point.

Adrian Flynn

Dramascripts

Orpheus and Eurydice

Dramatised by
ADRIAN FLYNN

1

WHERE THE TALE COMES FROM

This play is based on one of the many myths which were told by the Ancient Greeks. These were a people who lived in the area that is now modern Greece and the west coast of Turkey. Their civilisation was at its peak around two and a half thousand years ago, when they produced great philosophers, playwrights and law-givers. Much of what the ancient Greeks achieved then laid the foundations for life in western societies today.

The story of Orpheus, who legend says was the finest musician in Greece, is well-known. His journey into the underworld, trying to bring his wife Eurydice back from the dead, has been used as the basis for a number of films and at least two operas. Each generation seems to update the story. In this version, it is used to look at a very contemporary danger.

As the play begins, Orpheus, the pop star, is due to return from a concert tour. It is a chance to be reunited with his newly-wed wife, Eurydice. But will she still be waiting for him . . . ?

THE CHARACTERS

(in order of appearance)

FIRST FAN

SECOND FAN

ORPHEUS *a musician.*

JASON *his manager.*

CHARON *the doorman at the Tartarus night-club.*

CERBERUS *a barman.*

ARISTAEUS *a friend of Orpheus.*

MINOS

AEACUS   *The Judges of the Dead, Hades's bodyguards.*

RHADAMANTHYS

HADES *the owner of the night-club.*

EURYDICE *Orpheus's wife.*

OTHER CUSTOMERS*

* *indicates non-speaking parts*

Orpheus and Eurydice

Scene 1

The street outside ORPHEUS's flat.
Two of his FANS are waiting for ORPHEUS to arrive. They are reading a fan magazine.

1st FAN	*(Reading.)* Isn't it romantic?	1
2nd FAN	*(Reading.)* Orpheus is finally going to be reunited with his wife . . .	
1st FAN	*(Reading.)* . . . After tonight's concert.	
2nd FAN	*(Looking up.)* Still, it does seem weird. Them not even having a honeymoon together.	
1st FAN	It was in Orpheus's contract. He had a tour to play, marriage or no marriage.	
2nd FAN	I bet he can't wait to get back with . . . what's her name?	
1st FAN	*(Consults magazine.)* Eurydice.	10
2nd FAN	Eurydice? Good name for a musician's wife. Exotic and mysterious.	
1st FAN	*(Reading.)* It says, 'While top sax player Orpheus completes his set of concerts, wife Eurydice has been left at home.' Ooh.	

 **Eurydice** *Pronounced 'Yur-rid-a-see'.*

2ND FAN	What?
1ST FAN	*(Reading.)* Apparently, while Orpheus has been away, Eurydice has been seen in the company of one of his friends, Aristaeus.
2ND FAN	So?
1ST FAN	Maybe Aristaeus and Eurydice have got a thing going.
2ND FAN	Get out of here! Why would the wife of the best musician in town want anything to do with a dopehead like Aristaeus?
1ST FAN	*(Looking offstage.)* Look!
2ND FAN	*(Looking offstage.)* Orpheus!
1ST FAN	I told you it was worth waiting.
2ND FAN	Oh, wow!
1ST FAN	He always comes to his flat before a concert.
2ND FAN	Now, we've got to act cool. Silly, hysterical fans probably drive him crazy.
1ST FAN	Right.
	(ORPHEUS, carrying a saxophone, comes on. FANS rush excitedly over to him.)
2ND FAN	Wow, Orpheus, it's really you!
1ST FAN	I think you're fantastic!
ORPHEUS	Thanks.
2ND FAN	*(Quietly to 1st FAN.)* We've got to be cool, remember?

20

30

Aristaeus *Pronounced 'Aris-tay-us'. In the original myth, Aristaeus was very attracted to Eurydice.*

dopehead *Drug user.*

1ST FAN	*(Quietly.)* Right.
ORPHEUS	Have you two been waiting specially to see me?
2ND FAN	Oh no . . .
1ST FAN	No, no . . .
2ND FAN	We happened to be passing, that's all.
ORPHEUS	I was just going to call in at my flat, before I play tonight's concert.
1ST FAN	I think we might be going to that concert.
ORPHEUS	The truth is, I'm hoping my wife's at home. I've not seen her since I got back to town.
2ND FAN	I'm afraid she isn't.
ORPHEUS	No?
1ST FAN	Eurydice hasn't been home all day.
	(ORPHEUS gives the FANS a puzzled look.)
2ND FAN	We were just passing your house . . .
1ST FAN	All day. We've been here since this morning.
ORPHEUS	She must have gone straight to the concert hall. *(Looks offstage.)* My manager'll know.
	(JASON enters.)
JASON	Isn't she here?
ORPHEUS	These guys say she isn't. Couldn't you find her?
JASON	*(Worried.)* Ah.
ORPHEUS	What?
JASON	I heard a rumour.
2ND FAN	*(Quietly to 1st FAN.)* I hope it isn't the rumour we heard.
ORPHEUS	What kind of rumour?

40

50

60

7

JASON	Well . . .
ORPHEUS	Yes?
JASON	Some people think they've seen Eurydice in Tartarus.
ORPHEUS	What's Tartarus?
1ST FAN	It's a new night-club that opened while you were out of town.

70

JASON	And it's got a bad reputation.
2ND FAN	It's where all the deadbeats go.
1ST FAN	And the junkies.
ORPHEUS	Eurydice wouldn't go there. No way.
JASON	I heard that's where she is now.
ORPHEUS	Come on, Jason.
JASON	What are we going to do?
ORPHEUS	Get her out of there. (*He starts to go offstage.*)
1ST FAN	But Orpheus!
2ND FAN	What about tonight's concert?

80

| ORPHEUS | There's no concert till I get my wife back. |

ORPHEUS goes offstage, followed by JASON. The FANS go off, sorrowfully.

Tartarus *In Greek myth, Tartarus was the name given to the underworld, where the ghosts of the dead went.*

IMPROVISATION: Imagine Orpheus is being interviewed by his fans on television. They ask about his personal and professional life. Act the interview out, deciding whether it goes well, or whether Orpheus becomes annoyed with some of the questions.

SCENE 2

The entrance to the Tartarus Night-club. CHARON, the bouncer, is sending a CUSTOMER away.

CHARON	You ain't coming in. You ain't dressed right, you ain't our type. To get into Tartarus you've got to look dead sharp. So beat it.	1

(Disappointed, the CUSTOMER goes off. CHARON flexes his muscles, as ORPHEUS and JASON come on.)

ORPHEUS   What a dive!

JASON   Let me go in and check.

ORPHEUS   I'm going in. *(He tries to walk past CHARON.)*

CHARON   *(Grabs ORPHEUS by the arm.)* Hold it, buddy. No one gets into Tartarus without my say-so.   10

ORPHEUS   I've got to see if my wife's in there.

CHARON   Yeah, yeah. Everyone's got a story. You're not going in.

JASON   Don't you know who this is? This is Orpheus.

CHARON   Is that so?

JASON   The biggest musician in town.

CHARON   *(Sarcastically.)* Sure. And I'm the Captain of an Ocean Liner. Can't you see all the waves?

Charon Charon was a ferryman who would let the dead cross the River Styx to come into Tartarus. They had to pay him with a coin that had been buried with them.

dive Cheap and nasty looking club.

ORPHEUS	I really am Orpheus.
CHARON	So prove it.
	(ORPHEUS puts his saxophone to his mouth and plays a few, soulful notes.) 20
JASON	See?
CHARON	Maybe you are who you say you are.
ORPHEUS	Can I go in?
CHARON	I'll let you into the first bar, the Asphodel Bar.
ORPHEUS	That's a start.
CHARON	After that, it ain't up to me.
ORPHEUS	Thanks for your help.
CHARON	Usually folks slip me a coin or two when I help them get in.
ORPHEUS	*(Tries to find his wallet.)* Oh, right. 30
CHARON	But in your case, the music was enough. In you go.
ORPHEUS	Great.
	(ORPHEUS goes through the entrance and then offstage. JASON tries to follow him, but CHARON stops him.)
CHARON	Musicians, yes. Geeks, no.
	CHARON escorts JASON off the other side.

Asphodel *The Asphodel Fields were the first part of Tartarus. Those people who had been neither very good, nor very bad in life stayed here.*

geeks *Slang for a boring or dull person.*

MIME AND MOVEMENT: Using a suitable piece of music, show a Saturday night scene at the entrance to a night-club. Think about the types of people who might want to get in. The bouncers have to decide who succeeds and who stays out. Maybe someone tries to sneak in. Remember, people often have very distinctive ways of standing and moving when they're having a night out – they want to look their best.

SCENE 3

The Asphodel Bar.

CERBERUS, the barman, is polishing a glass. ARISTAEUS is slumped in a corner, drunk or drugged. There may be other CUSTOMERS sprawled around.

ORPHEUS comes in and goes up to CERBERUS.

CERBERUS	What can I get you?	1
ORPHEUS	Some information.	
CERBERUS	I'm a barman. I don't do information.	
ORPHEUS	Is my wife here? She's called Eurydice.	
CERBERUS	If you don't see her, she ain't here.	
ORPHEUS	Is she anywhere else in the building? In one of the other bars?	
CERBERUS	Like I say. I don't do information.	
	(CERBERUS goes back to polishing the glass. ORPHEUS desperately looks round the bar. He sees ARISTAEUS and goes over.)	10
ORPHEUS	Aristaeus! *(Grabs ARISTAEUS by the collar.)* Where is she?	
ARISTAEUS	*(Muddled.)* What?	
ORPHEUS	Where's Eurydice?	
ARISTAEUS	I don't know.	
ORPHEUS	I told you to look after her while I was away.	

 **Cerberus** *Cerberus was a three-headed dog who guarded Tartarus from intruders.*

ARISTAEUS	I've been busy.
ORPHEUS	*(Shakes ARISTAEUS.)* Where is she?
	(CERBERUS looks across at them.)
ARISTAEUS	Ssh! Don't get the barman mad.
ORPHEUS	I don't care about the barman.
ARISTAEUS	You ought to. That Cerberus is a headcase. Barking mad.
ORPHEUS	I want to know about Eurydice. Did you bring her here?
ARISTAEUS	She might have followed me in.
ORPHEUS	Is she here now?
ARISTAEUS	Maybe.
ORPHEUS	*(Drags ARISTAEUS to his feet.)* Tell me! Where's Eurydice!
ARISTAEUS	I think the owner of the club got interested in her.
	(CERBERUS takes hold of ORPHEUS's shoulder and pulls him away.)
CERBERUS	Get out of my bar now.
ORPHEUS	*(Frees himself.)* I'm not leaving here without my wife.

20

30

CERBERUS	Oh, aren't you?
ORPHEUS	No. I want to see the owner. He knows where she is.
CERBERUS	You're seeing no one. I'm throwing you out.
ORPHEUS	Your boss won't be too happy if you do.
CERBERUS	Hades, my boss, is perfectly happy with the way I do my job.
ORPHEUS	Not this time.
CERBERUS	How do you make that out?

40

ORPHEUS	Throwing the best sax player in the land out? He'll be mad with you.
ARISTAEUS	Orpheus is the best.
CERBERUS	I know Hades does like his music.

(ORPHEUS puts the sax to his mouth and plays a couple of bars. ARISTAEUS and other CUSTOMERS clap.)

ORPHEUS	Well?
CERBERUS	That's good playing.
ORPHEUS	Now can I see Hades?
CERBERUS	I tell you what. I'll take you to his bodyguards. I think they might know something about your wife.

50

ORPHEUS	What?
CERBERUS	Ask them. That's the best I can do.
ORPHEUS	OK. (Turns to ARISTAEUS.) I'll deal with you later.

(ARISTAEUS slinks off.)

| CERBERUS | This way. |

CERBERUS leads ORPHEUS off. Any other CUSTOMERS also go off.

SCENE 4

Outside HADES's office. The Three Judges of the Dead, MINOS, RHADAMANTHYS and AEACUS guard the door, checking their blackjacks and knuckle-dusters.

MINOS	The boss is in a hell of a mood tonight.	1
RHADAMANTHYS	So what's new?	
AEACUS	It seems his new secretary isn't happy here.	
RHADAMANTHYS	Who is?	
MINOS	If you want to be happy, you want to work in that other night-club.	
AEACUS	Do you mean the Elysium Club?	
MINOS	That's the one.	
RHADAMANTHYS	I wouldn't want to work there.	
AEACUS	No?	10
RHADAMANTHYS	That's where all the goody-goodies go.	

(ORPHEUS comes on. MINOS, RHADAMANTHYS and AEACUS stare at him, ready to attack at any moment. ORPHEUS looks terrified.)

ORPHEUS	*(Squeaky.)* Hi.
RHADAMANTHYS	*(Sinister.)* How exactly can we help?
ORPHEUS	The barman said your boss was through here.

Hades Hades was the god who ruled Tartarus.

The Judges of the Dead These three would judge new arrivals and decide if they should be sent to the punishment fields, back to the Asphodel Fields or, if the new arrival had been very good, on to the Elysium Fields.

Aeacus Pronounced 'Ay-arc-us'.

(*The JUDGES circle ORPHEUS.*)

MINOS	Hades? That's right. This is his office.
ORPHEUS	I must see him.
AEACUS	'Must' see him, must you?
ORPHEUS	Yes.
RHADAMANTHYS	The boss don't have to see no one.
MINOS	He sees who he wants to see, that's all.
AEACUS	Understand?
ORPHEUS	I think he's got my wife here, some kind of prisoner.
RHADAMANTHYS	Now isn't that sad?
AEACUS	Oh dear.
ORPHEUS	And if he won't let her go, I'll get the police.
MINOS	(*Laughs.*) Police?
RHADAMANTHYS	(*Laughs.*) Go right ahead.
AEACUS	(*Laughs.*) You can get the police, but don't you know who we are?
MINOS	We're the Judges.
ORPHEUS	Judges?
RHADAMANTHYS	Judge Rhadamanthys.
MINOS	Judge Minos.
AEACUS	Judge Aeacus.
MINOS	We judge which way you go.
AEACUS	This way, to the boss, if you're evil enough to be interesting.
MINOS	That way, back to the Asphodel Bar, if you're just another mediocrity.

20

30

40

RHADAMANTHYS	The lushes and the dopeheads, that is.
AEACUS	And the real creepy types . . .
MINOS	The ones who don't steal . . .
RHADAMANTHYS	Who don't cheat . . .
AEACUS	Who don't do drugs . . .
MINOS	We throw right back out on the street.
AEACUS	We tell them to go to Elysium. That's their kind of night-club.
ORPHEUS	Which way did you send my wife? *(The JUDGES look at each other.)* Please! I must know.
AEACUS	*(Tut-tuts.)* That 'must' word again.
ORPHEUS	I've only just married her. I'm going out of my mind.
RHADAMANTHYS	We'll think about it.
ORPHEUS	Eurydice doesn't belong in a place like this.
MINOS	And while we're thinking . . .
AEACUS	Let's hear a little music, sax-man.

50

(ORPHEUS plays a few bars. The JUDGES look at each other again. MINOS and RHADAMANTHYS nod at AEACUS.)

60

(Calls.) Boss! There's someone to see you.

 lushes   *People who drink too much alcohol.*

 ACTING: Although Orpheus is desperate to find his wife, the three judges are very frightening figures. Act this scene out, emphasising how much in control the judges are, both in their way of speaking and in their movement.

17

SCENE 5

HADES's office. EURYDICE is holding a notepad and pen. She's been taking dictation from HADES.

HADES	I don't want you around when this guy comes in.	1
EURYDICE	Who is he?	
HADES	It doesn't matter. Go and wait in the small office.	
	(EURYDICE goes offstage.)	
AEACUS	*(Offstage, calling.)* Boss! Can this guy come in yet?	
HADES	Send him in.	
	(ORPHEUS comes into the room.)	
ORPHEUS	You're Hades, are you?	
HADES	Mr Hades to you. What do you want?	
ORPHEUS	I want my wife back.	10
HADES	Your wife?	
ORPHEUS	Eurydice.	
HADES	Never heard of her.	
ORPHEUS	She came into the club with Aristaeus.	
HADES	That junkie?	
ORPHEUS	He doesn't know where she is now.	
HADES	Aristaeus doesn't know what day it is, let alone where his friends are.	
ORPHEUS	But your bodyguards told me you might know.	
HADES	Time I changed my bodyguards.	20

ORPHEUS	Where is she?
HADES	*(Shrugs.)* A lot of women come in this club. I can't remember all of them.
ORPHEUS	You'd know my wife. She's not a drug user or a drinker. She doesn't belong in a place like this.
HADES	That's what everyone says.
ORPHEUS	It's true. *(Calls.)* Eurydice! Are you here?
HADES	Hey, cut that out!
ORPHEUS	*(Calls.)* Eurydice!

(EURYDICE runs on.)   **30**

EURYDICE	Orpheus! I knew you'd find me.
HADES	I told you to stay out of here.
ORPHEUS	*(Puts his arm round EURYDICE.)* You can't keep me from my wife.
HADES	Can't I?
ORPHEUS	No. *(To EURYDICE.)* We're getting out of here straightaway.
HADES	What if I won't let her go?
ORPHEUS	You can't keep her here.
HADES	Maybe Eurydice doesn't want to go.
ORPHEUS	*(To EURYDICE.)* Of course you do, don't you? **40**
EURYDICE	Orpheus, there's something you don't know.
HADES	This perfect wife of yours is actually a junkie herself.
ORPHEUS	A junkie? Don't make me laugh.
HADES	I'm not trying to. It's the simple truth.
EURYDICE	He's right, Orpheus.
ORPHEUS	You can't be!

19

HADES	She wouldn't be able to cope with life outside Tartarus any more. Here she gets what she needs.
ORPHEUS	Eurydice, I don't believe it.
EURYDICE	I'm sorry. I'm an addict.
ORPHEUS	How? How did it happen?
EURYDICE	It started when you went away.
ORPHEUS	I should never have gone on tour!
EURYDICE	Aristaeus was trying to look after me, like you'd asked him to. Just keeping me company at first.
HADES	Nasty piece of work, that Aristaeus.
EURYDICE	We'd come here. Sit in the bar for hours. I didn't enjoy it much, but I thought, soon you'd be back in town and life would become normal again. Only Aristaeus started to get ideas.
ORPHEUS	What ideas?
EURYDICE	He wanted to be my lover.
ORPHEUS	I'll kill him!
HADES	No need. With what he's putting in his bloodstream, he'll kill himself.
EURYDICE	To get away from him, I started sitting with some of the other guys here. Big mistake.
ORPHEUS	What happened?
EURYDICE	They spent their whole time taking stuff. At first I didn't know what they were taking. At least, I pretended not to know. But I knew all right. And then, just to fit in, I started taking it myself. It's poison.

50

60

70

HADES	Heartbreaking, how easy it is to get hooked.
ORPHEUS	You started taking drugs?
EURYDICE	Now I don't think I can do without them.
HADES	She wouldn't last a day outside here.
ORPHEUS	I can't go back without you.
EURYDICE	You'll have to.
ORPHEUS	No!
HADES	She can't go with you. Not possible.
EURYDICE	Orpheus, there's one thing I want. Before you leave.
ORPHEUS	Anything.
EURYDICE	Do you remember the first time I saw you, when you weren't a big star? You were busking on the street.
ORPHEUS	Of course I remember. It was a horrible day. It wouldn't stop raining.
EURYDICE	I was the only person who stood and watched you. I didn't care about the rain. The song you were playing was so beautiful. Play it for a last time, Orpheus.
	(ORPHEUS plays part of a slow, sad tune on the saxophone. When it finishes, he and EURYDICE cling to each other.)
HADES	That instrument is bewitched.
ORPHEUS	Can't we even be alone to say goodbye?

80

90

poison *In the original myth, Aristaeus tried to assault Eurydice sexually. Getting away from him, Eurydice was bitten by a snake and died of the poison.*

hooked *Addicted to drugs.*

busking *Playing music and hoping passers-by will throw you some money for it.*

HADES	You're not saying goodbye.
EURYDICE	What?
HADES	I've not done this before, I won't do it again. I'm letting you go, Eurydice.
ORPHEUS	You are?
HADES	There's something special in the music. I don't know what.
EURYDICE	How can I leave? You said I won't last a day on the outside. **100**
HADES	You're pretty badly hooked, but I reckon if you go now, you've got a chance.

EURYDICE	You really think so?
HADES	It'll be a nightmare at first, kicking the habit. But you'll manage. Orpheus, she can leave with you.
ORPHEUS	Thanks, Mr Hades.
HADES	On one condition.
ORPHEUS	What's that?
HADES	You've got to walk out of here first, on your own. You go past my bodyguards, through the bar and out the door, without once looking back.
ORPHEUS	What?
HADES	Don't turn round. Don't check to see if your wife's following you.
ORPHEUS	Why not?
HADES	That's the condition.
EURYDICE	You've got to trust me, Orpheus. You've got to believe I'm strong enough to leave here by myself.
HADES	If you start doubting whether she's behind you or not, you're never going to trust her again. Every day you'll wonder, 'Is she still taking drugs? Is she a junkie again?' Without trust, you'll make her life outside a worse hell than in here.
ORPHEUS	Of course I trust you, Eurydice.
EURYDICE	You must do.
HADES	Turn back once, and you've lost her. Agreed? *(He holds out his hand.)*
ORPHEUS	Agreed. *(He shakes HADES's hand.)*
HADES	Now get moving before I change my mind.

110

120

DISCUSSION: In small groups, look at Eurydice's explanation for why she started to take drugs. Does it seem believable? What other reasons have you heard people give for taking drugs? What do you know of the difficulties of overcoming drug addiction? Why do you think Eurydice places so much importance on Orpheus being able to trust her?

IMPROVISATION: Look again at how Orpheus and Eurydice first met. Improvise this scene, up to a point where they agree to meet again.

FREEZE-FRAME: Freeze the action where Hades and Orpheus are shaking hands, while Eurydice looks on. Have other people speak their thoughts and feelings at that moment.

SCENE 6

The whole of the Tartarus night-club.

AEACUS, MINOS and RHADAMANTHYS take up bodyguard duty at one side of the stage. CERBERUS stands polishing glasses in the middle of the stage. ARISTAEUS slouches on a bar stool next to him. Any other CUSTOMERS stand near them. CHARON stands at the other side of the stage, stopping JASON from entering the club.

Music is heard, as ORPHEUS comes on stage. He nods at the JUDGES, before going into the bar. CERBERUS, surprised to see him back, stops polishing for a moment. ARISTAEUS looks at ORPHEUS for a moment, then turns away embarrassed.

EURYDICE comes on, some way behind ORPHEUS. Silently, the JUDGES bid her goodbye. ORPHEUS is tempted to look back, but doesn't. He walks towards the entrance and comes out. EURYDICE goes to silently say goodbye to CERBERUS.

The music fades down.

JASON	I didn't think you were coming out.	1
ORPHEUS	Neither did I.	
JASON	Did you find her?	
ORPHEUS	Yes.	
JASON	Where is she?	
ORPHEUS ·	*(Starts to turn round, then stops himself.)* She's following me.	
JASON	Is she?	
ORPHEUS	She's just a little way behind.	
JASON	Are you sure?	
ORPHEUS	Yes. She's right behind me.	10

JASON	If you say so, Orpheus. I can't see her.
	(EURYDICE finishes saying goodbye to CERBERUS, and starts walking towards the entrance.)
ORPHEUS	Maybe she's having second thoughts. Maybe she doesn't love me enough. *(He turns round and sees EURYDICE following him. She is almost at the door. He reaches out his hand for her.)* Quick! You've almost made it.
	(HADES comes onstage behind ORPHEUS. EURYDICE becomes still.)
HADES	You looked back.
ORPHEUS	No.
HADES	You didn't trust her enough, so you turned your head.
	(MINOS, RHADAMANTHYS and AEACUS slowly walk up to EURYDICE and take hold of her.)
ORPHEUS	I didn't! I didn't mean to . . . I couldn't help myself.
HADES	Remember our agreement?
ORPHEUS	Please! She was almost in my arms.
	(HADES walks past ORPHEUS.)
HADES	*(To CHARON.)* Lock up for the night.
CHARON	Sir.
ORPHEUS	You've got to let me back in.
CHARON	*(Puts his hand up very firmly.)* Sorry. We're closed.
HADES	You heard the man.
	(The JUDGES lead EURYDICE off. JASON puts his hand on ORPHEUS's shoulder.)
JASON	It's too late.
ORPHEUS	*(Calls.)* Eurydice! Eurydice!

20

30

SHADOWING: In pairs, one person follows the other around the room, copying their movements. As soon as the leader stops moving, the follower must stop. If the follower doesn't stop quickly enough, they have to take over as leader.

HOT-SEATING: In small groups, ask Orpheus and Eurydice what their thoughts were when they realised they were going to be separated for ever.

SCENE 7

The street outside ORPHEUS's flat. The two FANS are waiting, looking at a fan magazine.

1ST FAN	It says here, Orpheus has been back to the Tartarus night-club every night for a month, but it's always closed.
2ND FAN	I don't think he's been the same since he lost Eurydice. You know what I mean?
1ST FAN	He doesn't play as good?
2ND FAN	Doesn't seem to.
1ST FAN	And it's boring hanging round his flat all the time.
2ND FAN	I bet we don't see him again . . .
1ST FAN	Isn't he going on tour with his manager's group now? What's it called?
2ND FAN	*(Looks at magazine.)* 'Jason and the Argonauts'.
1ST FAN	Always have to call themselves something daft.
2ND FAN	*(Looks at magazine.)* Here's someone new.
1ST FAN	Who's that?
2ND FAN	Pan.
1ST FAN	*(Looks at magazine.)* Funny looking legs.

1

10

Jason and the Argonauts *In another Greek myth, Orpheus joined the hero Jason on his ship, 'The Argo' to go in search of a golden fleece.*

Pan *A Greek god, who was half-man and half-goat. He played a set of pipes.*

2ND FAN	He's meant to be brilliant on the pipes, though.	
1ST FAN	Is he?	
2ND FAN	Might be worth a listen.	
1ST FAN	Shall we go and sit outside his house all day?	20
2ND FAN	You're on.	

The two FANS go offstage.

DISCUSSION: Read this traditional account of Orpheus and Eurydice, which comes from *Of Heroes, Gods and Men* by Robert Graves: Orpheus . . . was the most famous poet and musician who ever lived . . . After a visit to Egypt, Orpheus . . . married Eurydice. One day . . . Eurydice met Aristaeus who tried to force her. She trod on a serpent as she fled, and died of its bite; but Orpheus boldly descended into Tartarus, hoping to fetch her back. On his arrival, he not only charmed the ferryman Charon, the dog Cerberus, and the three Judges of the Dead with his plaintive music, but temporarily suspended the tortures of the damned; and so far soothed the savage heart of Hades that he won leave to restore Eurydice to the upper world. Hades made a single condition: that Orpheus might not look behind him until she was safely back under the light of the sun. Eurydice followed Orpheus up through the dark passage, guided by the sounds of his lyre, and it was only when he reached the sunlight again that he turned to see whether she were still behind him, and so lost her for ever.

How closely does the play follow the original story? What are the main differences?

Why do you think the playwright decided to set the play in the present day, rather than in Ancient Greece?

DISCUSSION: In the end, Orpheus just fails to rescue Eurydice. What is the biggest disappointment you have ever experienced? How close were you to achieving what you wanted?

PERFORMANCE: In small groups, choose one scene of the play to act. Think about the way each of the characters will be feeling in that scene, and how you can show that feeling in your movement, facial expression and voice.

STORYBOARDING: Storyboard what you think are the three most important moments in the play.

WRITING: Imagine you're a writer for a music paper. Write an article about Orpheus's music career, and the effect losing his wife has on it.

force *To sexually assault or rape.*

lyre *A stringed instrument.*

Dramascripts

Mr Mukherjee, Ghostcatcher

Dramatised by
ADRIAN FLYNN

WHERE THE TALE COMES FROM

The folk story this play is based on comes from Bengal – the region which covers the north-eastern corner of India and the whole of Bangladesh. There has always been a great tradition of oral story-telling in this area, with stories being passed on from one generation to the next. Over time, the details of the stories change to suit different times and different audiences.

A theme of many Bengali folk stories is the trickster who outwits a more powerful opponent by relying on cunning rather than strength. That is certainly how Mr Mukherjee tackles the two ghosts in this story. However, it is not just supernatural dangers Mr Mukherjee has to escape from. At the beginning of the play, he is trapped in a much more familiar situation . . .

THE CHARACTERS

BHARAT MUKHERJEE

MRS MUKHERJEE

CHANDRA *their son, aged 13.*

ASHA *their daughter, aged 17.*

UNCLE *a ghost.*

JUNIOR SPOOK

Mr Mukherjee, Ghostcatcher
Scene 1

T he *MUKHERJEES' house. MRS MUKHERJEE is alone onstage, next to a dining table. She looks at her watch.*

MRS MUKHERJEE	*(Quietly.)* It's early morning. Seven twenty-nine and fifty seconds. Everything in the house is peaceful. My husband is sleeping peacefully. My children are sleeping peacefully. *(Rubs her hands gleefully.)* Well, we'll soon change all that. *(Calls.)* Wake up everybody! You've got half an hour to get washed, have breakfast, do your teeth, clean your shoes, feed the hamster, find your maths homework, do your maths homework if you can't find it, pack your gym kit and be ready for school or work. *(The two Mukherjee children, ASHA and CHANDRA, rush across the stage to get to the bathroom. ASHA wins the race.)*	1 10
CHANDRA	*(Comes to breakfast table.)* How come Asha always gets to the bathroom first?	
MRS MUKHERJEE	Cereal, cereal and toast, or just toast?	
CHANDRA	Toast.	
	(MRS MUKHERJEE serves CHANDRA's breakfast, as MR MUKHERJEE comes onstage and goes to the bathroom door.)	
MR MUKHERJEE	Asha, dear?	
ASHA	*(Offstage.)* What?	
MR MUKHERJEE	Are you going to be in there long?	20
ASHA	*(Offstage.)* No.	

MR MUKHERJEE	Good. You see, today's a very important day at work.
ASHA	*(Offstage.)* I'm washing my hair, that's all.
MR MUKHERJEE	Washing your hair? *(He shakes his head sadly and comes to the breakfast table.)* I'll never get in the bathroom.
CHANDRA	Dad, I need some money . . .
MRS MUKHERJEE	Cereal, cereal and toast, or just toast?
CHANDRA	. . . for some new trainers.
MRS MUKHERJEE	Well?
MR MUKHERJEE	Just toast.
CHANDRA	Everyone else in my class has got new trainers.
MR MUKHERJEE	You bought some last week.
MRS MUKHERJEE	There isn't any toast left. Chandra's had it all.
CHANDRA	Those trainers are rubbish.
MR MUKHERJEE	I'll have cereal then.
CHANDRA	They're completely out of fashion. I'll be a laughing-stock if I wear them to school.
MRS MUKHERJEE	I'm saving the cereal for Asha. You'll have to do without breakfast.
MR MUKHERJEE	Oh dear.
CHANDRA	Plus there's this brilliant new computer game I've got to have.
MRS MUKHERJEE	If you gave me enough money for the housekeeping, we'd have enough cereal and toast for everyone.
CHANDRA	All my friends have got it.
MR MUKHERJEE	I don't have any spare money at the moment.
CHANDRA	Dad!

30

40

MRS MUKHERJEE	Typical! My mother warned me.
CHANDRA	If I don't get this game, I'm nobody. Everyone's got it.
MRS MUKHERJEE	She said, 'Marry that man and you'll live to regret it.' Did I listen to her? No. 50
MR MUKHERJEE	But, you see, today's a very important day at work . . .
MRS MUKHERJEE	How I wish I'd listened to her.
CHANDRA	If I can't have the computer game, at least give me the money for a new CD.
MRS MUKHERJEE	There were lots of men who wanted to marry me. I could have had my pick of the bunch . . .
CHANDRA	Come on Dad.
MRS MUKHERJEE	. . . I could be living in a beautiful house, with a butler and maids. Instead of which, I married you. Huh! 60
MR MUKHERJEE	The truth is, when I've shown my new invention at work, I hope . . .
CHANDRA	Can I have some money?
MRS MUKHERJEE	I've been too soft-hearted for my own good, that's the trouble.
MR MUKHERJEE	. . . with any luck they'll give me a raise.
CHANDRA	Cash, right now please.
MRS MUKHERJEE	It's no use asking your father for money. He's a complete non-achiever, just like my mother said he'd be.
	(ASHA comes onstage, drying her hair.) 70
ASHA	Is breakfast ready?
MR MUKHERJEE	Are you finished with the bathroom, dear? *(CHANDRA rushes offstage to the bathroom.)* Never mind.
MRS MUKHERJEE	Come and have your cereal, Asha. I can't offer you any toast, because your father has wolfed it all.

MR MUKHERJEE	I haven't eaten anything.
ASHA	Dad, I need some new clothes for a party.
MRS MUKHERJEE	My mother warned me not to marry him, but did I listen?
ASHA	Not a lot of money. Just enough for a complete new outfit.
MRS MUKHERJEE	No I didn't, and I've regretted it every day since then.
MR MUKHERJEE	*(Opens his bag.)* I'm hoping, when I show my boss my new improved mirror . . .
ASHA	And I'll need some money for a taxi to get me home from the party . . .
MRS MUKHERJEE	Though I've never uttered a word of complaint.
ASHA	. . . plus, of course, money for a taxi to get me to the party. And a few pounds to buy a present. And what else will I need?

80

MR MUKHERJEE	*(Stands up.)* I'm sorry my dears, I've had enough.
MRS MUKHERJEE	*(Takes no notice of her husband.)* That's my biggest fault . . . **90**
ASHA	*(Taking no notice of her father.)* I absolutely must have a new handbag.
MR MUKHERJEE	I'm serious. I'm leaving. And I'm never coming back.
	(MR MUKHERJEE leaves the table, taking his bag, and goes to the side of the stage. Neither MRS MUKHERJEE nor ASHA take any notice.)
MRS MUKHERJEE	. . . I'm too uncomplaining. That's what my mother always said.
ASHA	Obviously I'm going to get my hair done before I go and that won't be cheap. **100**
MR MUKHERJEE	Goodbye. *(He goes off.)*
MRS MUKHERJEE	Other women would have made their husband's life a misery, asking for this, asking for that.
ASHA	But I'll get a manicure at the same time and they give you a special rate if they do your hair and your hands.
MRS MUKHERJEE	Luckily, I'm not like that. No one's ever heard me complain about having a useless good-for-nothing husband.
CHANDRA	*(Coming back onstage.)* And Dad, I need some money to go to the cinema tomorrow. *(Looks around.)* Dad?
ASHA	Where's he gone? **110**
MRS MUKHERJEE	That's just typical. Your father has a big moan at all of us, then goes off without letting us get a word in edgeways.

 **get a word in edgeways** *Manage to speak while someone else is talking a lot.*

DISCUSSION: Mr Mukherjee finally decides he can't stand living at home any more. List the reasons why he is unhappy at home. What other reasons can make people want to escape from their family?

IMPROVISATION: This scene depends on the members of Mr Mukherjee's family talking so rapidly that he doesn't get the chance to be heard himself. In pairs, keep a conversation going for at least a minute, without any silent pauses. Don't worry if the conversation doesn't make much sense – the important thing is to avoid any gaps.

SCENE 2

The forest. JUNIOR SPOOK and UNCLE are to one side of the forest.

JUNIOR SPOOK	The thing is, Uncle . . .	1
UNCLE	Yes?	
JUNIOR SPOOK	. . . I want to resign.	
UNCLE	Resign?	
JUNIOR SPOOK	Yes.	
UNCLE	You can't resign from being a ghost. You just **are** a ghost.	
JUNIOR SPOOK	But I'm hopeless at it.	
UNCLE	You're not hopeless.	
JUNIOR SPOOK	I'm not scary enough.	
UNCLE	You're still learning your trade.	10
JUNIOR SPOOK	That old lady you sent me to haunt.	
UNCLE	What about her?	
JUNIOR SPOOK	She ended up patting me on the head and leaving out a saucer of milk for me every day.	
UNCLE	You just need some expert tuition.	
JUNIOR SPOOK	I don't think I'll ever be very frightening, Uncle.	
UNCLE	Listen, Junior Spook. No nephew of mine is going to fail as a ghost. You've got to realise humans frighten very easily.	

 **expert tuition** *Teaching from someone who knows a lot about the subject.*

JUNIOR SPOOK	No they don't.
UNCLE	They do. They're full of superstitions and crazy ideas. Why, **20** they're even afraid of the dark.
JUNIOR SPOOK	Will you show me how to frighten them?
UNCLE	That's just what I'm going to do. Let's take a walk in the forest and see who we can scare.

(JUNIOR SPOOK and UNCLE go off, as MR MUKHERJEE comes on with his bag.)

MR MUKHERJEE   *(To himself.)* Finally I've escaped. No more 'Dad I want this, Dad I want that.' No more 'Why didn't I listen to my mother?' From now on, there's just going to be peace and quiet. Under this tree looks the perfect place to start my   **30** new life.

(He sits down. He opens his bag, takes the mirror out and looks in it.) You're getting grey hairs, Bharat Mukherjee. *(Stops looking in the mirror.)* Suppose I had gone to work and shown the boss my new improved mirror. Suppose he'd given me a great big pay-rise. My family would nag at me all day and all night until they'd got all the extra money. And they still wouldn't be happy. No, the mirror is best kept here. *(He puts it back in the bag, which he closes.)* And I'm better off staying in this nice, shady forest, having a   **40** little snooze.

(He pulls his hat over his eyes, as he leans back to have a nap. JUNIOR SPOOK and UNCLE come back on, quite close to MR MUKHERJEE.)

UNCLE   Are you all right now?

 **superstitions** *Illogical beliefs, usually based on ignorance or fear.*

JUNIOR SPOOK	I'm fine, Uncle.
UNCLE	It was only a squirrel.
JUNIOR SPOOK	I know.
UNCLE	Then you shouldn't have screamed when you saw it.
JUNIOR SPOOK	(*Nervously points to MR MUKHERJEE.*) Uncle, look. A human.
UNCLE	Perfect.
JUNIOR SPOOK	He looks a bit scary.
UNCLE	You're going to scare him.
JUNIOR SPOOK	Me? How?
UNCLE	Creep up on him.
JUNIOR SPOOK	(*Writes it down in a notebook.*) Creep up on him.
UNCLE	Emit a blood-curdling howl.
JUNIOR SPOOK	(*Writing.*) Blood-curdling howl . . .
UNCLE	Then walk round him, like you're rattling heavy chains.
JUNIOR SPOOK	(*Writing.*) Heavy chains. Got it!
UNCLE	He'll be frightened out of his mind. I'm going to wait behind this tree and see how you get on.

50

60

(*UNCLE sneaks behind a nearby tree. JUNIOR SPOOK checks his notes nervously. UNCLE gives a big thumbs-up sign. JUNIOR SPOOK creeps up on MR MUKHERJEE and lets out a feeble scream. MR MUKHERJEE stays asleep.*)

(*JUNIOR SPOOK looks to his UNCLE for help. UNCLE signals him to creep round another way. JUNIOR SPOOK does so, and lets out another feeble scream. Nothing happens.*)

emit *Here it means, to make a sound.*

(JUNIOR SPOOK taps MR MUKHERJEE on the shoulder.)   70

JUNIOR SPOOK   Excuse me.

MR MUKHERJEE   (Sitting up and taking off his hat.) Can I help you?

JUNIOR SPOOK   Could you wake up for a moment . . .

MR MUKHERJEE   Certainly.

JUNIOR SPOOK   . . . so I can scare you out of your wits?

MR MUKHERJEE   Right-ho.

                      (JUNIOR SPOOK tries to make a blood-curdling scream.)

                      Have you started yet?

                      (JUNIOR SPOOK tries screaming again.)

                      Will you tell me when to be frightened?   80

JUNIOR SPOOK   You're not frightened now?

MR MUKHERJEE   No.

JUNIOR SPOOK   Just a moment. (He takes out his notebook, then shakes his head and goes over to his UNCLE.) I can't read my own handwriting.

UNCLE   Heavy chains.

JUNIOR SPOOK   Right. (He moves slowly back towards MR MUKHERJEE, making ghostly noises, and pretending to rattle heavy chains.)

MR MUKHERJEE   You don't look very comfortable. Are your trousers too tight?   90

JUNIOR SPOOK   You're still not frightened of me?

MR MUKHERJEE   No. Why should I be?

JUNIOR SPOOK   Because I'm a ghost.

MR MUKHERJEE   But I'm a ghost-catcher.

JUNIOR SPOOK   (Frightened.) A ghost-catcher?

MR MUKHERJEE   Yes. I make my living by going round catching silly little ghosts like you and putting them in my bag. *(He lifts up his bag.)*

JUNIOR SPOOK   You put ghosts in there?

MR MUKHERJEE   I've got one in here right now, as a matter of fact. Want to have a look?   100

JUNIOR SPOOK   A tiny, little look. *(MR MUKHERJEE opens his bag slightly. JUNIOR SPOOK creeps up nervously and takes a quick look. He screams.)* That ghost looks just like me!

MR MUKHERJEE	And you're going in the bag next.
JUNIOR SPOOK	Oh no, please no.
MR MUKHERJEE	You will. Unless you get me some of the things I want.
JUNIOR SPOOK	What things?
MR MUKHERJEE	Give me your notebook. I've got a list to write.

JUNIOR SPOOK gives MR MUKHERJEE his notebook, as the   **110**
lights come down on the forest.

DISCUSSION: Uncle says that humans have many superstitions. One example of a superstition is the belief that walking under ladders is unlucky. As a class, see how many different superstitions you can think of. How do you think these superstitions started?

WRITING: Different people are afraid of different things. Mr Mukherjee is not afraid of ghosts, but he does seem frightened of his family. Describe the things you are most afraid of, or the most frightening experience you have ever had.

DRAMA GAME: 'Stone Face'. Mr Mukherjee doesn't betray any emotion when the ghost tries to frighten him. Take turns in trying to make a partner smile or laugh, by pulling faces or making noises (but not touching).

SCENE 3

The MUKHERJEES' house. MRS MUKHERJEE, ASHA and CHANDRA are sitting round the dining-table, having dinner. They are incredibly polite and well-mannered towards each other.

MRS MUKHERJEE	Did you have a good day at school, dear?	1
CHANDRA	Yes, thank you, Mother.	
MRS MUKHERJEE	And what was your day like, Asha?	
ASHA	Fine, thank you. I'm really enjoying my new job.	
CHANDRA	Would you be so kind as to pass the salt, Mother?	
ASHA	I'll have it after you please, Chandra.	
MRS MUKHERJEE	*(Passing salt to CHANDRA.)* There you are, dear.	
CHANDRA	You have it first, Asha.	
ASHA	No, after you.	
CHANDRA	Please. I insist.	10
MRS MUKHERJEE	This is nice. A good, old-fashioned, family meal. But I can't help feeling . . .	
ASHA	What, Mother?	
MRS MUKHERJEE	. . . is there someone missing?	

ASHA, CHANDRA and MRS MUKHERJEE all try to remember who is missing.

Lights down on the MUKHERJEES' house.

DISCUSSION: When Mr Mukherjee isn't at home, the rest of his family behave differently from normal. In pairs, discuss whether you change the way you behave according to the people you are with. Are you different with your family, to the way you are with your friends? Do different friends bring out different sides of your personality?

SCENE 4

The forest. JUNIOR SPOOK is showing UNCLE his notebook, while MR MUKHERJEE is once again resting under his tree.

UNCLE	*(Angry.)* He wants a computer game?	1
JUNIOR SPOOK	And some CDs, and a voucher for the hairdresser, some new clothes . . .	
UNCLE	Junior Spook! You should be ashamed of yourself.	
JUNIOR SPOOK	And he wants more housekeeping money. Otherwise I'm going in his bag.	
UNCLE	A ghostcatcher indeed! I've never heard such nonsense.	
JUNIOR SPOOK	He is!	
UNCLE	I'll show you how to deal with him. Watch this.	
	(UNCLE moves towards MR MUKHERJEE, making a series of hideous sounds. MR MUKHERJEE sits up and smiles politely.)	10
	(To JUNIOR SPOOK.) I think this needs my extra-terrifying, heart-freezing moan. *(He gives a terrific moan.)*	
MR MUKHERJEE	Have you got a sore throat?	
UNCLE	*(To JUNIOR SPOOK.)* That's it! I'm going to have to use my 'Face of Maximum Terror.' It'll probably make his hair fall out and his ears drop off. *(He distorts his face into a hideous expression.)*	

 **distorts** Pulls out of its normal shape.

MR MUKHERJEE	I know! You've got toothache.	
UNCLE	Don't you realise I'm the most frightening sight in the whole country?	20
MR MUKHERJEE	You haven't seen my daughter dressed up for a party.	
JUNIOR SPOOK	Aren't you even a little bit scared of my uncle?	
MR MUKHERJEE	I told you. Ghostcatchers don't get scared.	
UNCLE	I don't believe in this ghostcatching business.	
MR MUKHERJEE	That's what I do.	
UNCLE	Maybe you can catch weedy little ghosts like my nephew . . .	
JUNIOR SPOOK	Oi!	
UNCLE	. . . but you could never catch a great, powerful ghost like me.	30
MR MUKHERJEE	As it happens, I've got a ghost just like you in my bag already.	
UNCLE	Impossible.	
MR MUKHERJEE	He's your spitting image. Want to have a look? *(Opens the bag a little.)*	
UNCLE	Maybe a tiny little look. *(He creeps up to the bag and looks in. He screams.)* He looks exactly like me!	
MR MUKHERJEE	And you're going into the bag next, unless . . .	
UNCLE	Junior!	
JUNIOR SPOOK	Yes, Uncle?	40
UNCLE	Where's the shopping list the nice man gave us?	

 **spitting image** *Someone who looks exactly the same.*

ARTWORK: Make a mask of the most frightening face you can imagine.

MIME: Act out this scene in mime, using movement, sounds and masks to show what is happening. Show the way the ghosts' attitude to Mr Mukherjee changes when he refuses to be frightened.

SCENE 5

The MUKHERJEES' house. MRS MUKHERJEE, ASHA and CHANDRA are sitting around the table.

MRS MUKHERJEE	It's been a lovely evening, hasn't it?	1
CHANDRA	I've enjoyed playing cards instead of sitting in front of my computer all night.	
ASHA	And I didn't really want to go to that party anyway.	
MRS MUKHERJEE	All the same, I can't help feeling something isn't quite right.	
CHANDRA	I know what you mean, Mother, but . . .	
ASHA	I can't work out what it is . . .	
	(MR MUKHERJEE comes into the house, carrying his now very heavy bag.)	10
MR MUKHERJEE	I was going to escape from you for good. But of my own free will I've decided to come back.	
MRS MUKHERJEE	That's what was missing!	
MR MUKHERJEE	I realised, when I was in the forest, that for all its faults, this is my home.	
ASHA	You've been in the forest?	
MRS MUKHERJEE	Typical! He'd rather talk to trees than to his own flesh and blood.	

flesh and blood *Family or relatives.*

CHANDRA	You should have been here, giving us our pocket money.	
ASHA	I couldn't go to my party, thanks to you.	20
CHANDRA	I had nothing to play on my computer.	
MR MUKHERJEE	Look. *(He opens his bag and starts to take things out.)* A new pair of trainers for Chandra. Party clothes for Asha. Some housekeeping money for you, Mrs Mukherjee.	
	(CHANDRA, ASHA and MRS MUKHERJEE come to collect their gifts.)	
CHANDRA	Wow!	
ASHA	Thanks, Dad.	
MR MUKHERJEE	*(Emptying the bag.)* There's computer games, fashionable new shoes, everything.	30
	(ASHA and CHANDRA inspect their gifts with delight.)	
MRS MUKHERJEE	You've brought all these presents back for us?	
MR MUKHERJEE	Of course. You only have to say what you want and I get it. Despite all the trouble you cause me, you are my family and this is where I belong.	
	(They all smile cheesily at each other for a moment. Then . . .)	
ASHA	*(Holding up a blouse or tee-shirt.)* You know, this top is really very nice, Dad.	
MR MUKHERJEE	I know.	
ASHA	But it's last year's colour.	40
CHANDRA	And this computer game's very good.	
MR MUKHERJEE	Good.	

 **smile cheesily** *They all give a big smile, but without really meaning it.*

CHANDRA	But there's a better one out now.
MRS MUKHERJEE	And it's all very well giving me a bit of extra housekeeping, Mr Mukherjee, but have you seen the latest price increases?
ASHA	Really, I need a top like this in red. And in gold. And in purple. And in pale blue with polka dots . . .
CHANDRA	*(Overlapping.)* Actually there are two games, no three games, no four games which are much, much better and I've got to have them all.

50

MRS MUKHERJEE	*(Overlapping.)* With the money you give me, you can't have fresh meat if you want fresh vegetables as well, let alone fresh fruit. And what about some fresh cream and milk . . .

(ASHA, CHANDRA and MRS MUKHERJEE carry on silently listing all the things they want. MR MUKHERJEE goes to the side of the stage.)

MR MUKHERJEE	*(To himself.)* I managed to tell them that I was leaving. And I've managed to tell them I've come back. I suppose I'll just have to be happy with that. *(He goes off.)*

ASHA	
CHANDRA }	And there's another thing!
MRS MUKHERJEE	

60

They freeze. Lights out.

DISCUSSION: For all his family's faults, Mr Mukherjee decided that he was better staying with them, rather than escaping from them. What are the good things you can get from living with a family?

IMPROVISATION: Imagine Mr Mukherjee finally shows his boss the new improved mirror he had in his bag. Prepare and act out a television advertisement for the mirror, highlighting its special new qualities.

WRITING: Write a training manual for newly-qualified ghosts, teaching them the best ways to terrify humans.

Dramascripts

Anansi and
the Moon

Dramatised by
ADRIAN FLYNN

WHERE THE TALE COMES FROM

This play is based on an Ashanti folktale. The Ashanti people live in Ghana, in West Africa, and they have a great tradition of story-telling. Many of these stories have animals as their hero, and one of the most popular of these heroes is Anansi the Spider. As the Ashanti people have travelled, they have carried their stories with them. Anansi stories are known and liked throughout the world, particularly in the Caribbean. In countries such as Jamaica, Anansi stories are still being rewritten and retold.

Anansi, like Mr Mukherjee, is a trickster – someone who gets what they want through brains, not brawn. In this story, however, Anansi is unable to get out of trouble on his own, and needs to call on the help of his family to escape from danger. But, as the play begins, Anansi is not in a very good mood with his children . . .

57

THE CHARACTERS

ANANSI

His children

ROAD BUILDER

RIVER DRINKER

CUSHION

GAME SKINNER

STONE THROWER

SEE DANGER

Although Anansi is a spider, he and his children are very human in character. The play can be read and performed as though they are ordinary people, if wished.

ANANSI AND THE MOON

PROLOGUE

A NANSI's house. ANANSI's six CHILDREN are throwing around a great white globe.

ANANSI	*(Raps directly to audience.)* My name's Anansi, I don't mean to intrude, But I'd like to introduce you, To the kids in my brood. You see I've got six, Who give me plenty trouble. Now speak for yourselves, And on the double!	1
ROAD BUILDER	I ain't Hilda, or Tilda, Or even Gilda. What you got to call me is . . .	10
EVERYBODY	Road Builder!	
RIVER DRINKER	My name is River Drinker, I'm a bad-assed dude.	
EVERYBODY	Can you say 'bad-ass' in class?	
ANANSI	I think that's rude!	

 **brood** *A group of young animals born at the same time.*

SEE DANGER	Now listen to me, I don't want to be a stranger. When I predict trouble, They call me . . .	20
EVERYBODY	See Danger!	
ANANSI	*(Quietly.)* Those three kids Can make me curse. The only problem is, The next three are worse.	
GAME SKINNER	*(Chants.)* Meat for my dinner! Meat for my dinner! I'm always out hunting, So they call me . . .	30
EVERYBODY	Game Skinner!	
STONE THROWER	I ain't Esau or Elijah Or even Noah. What you got to call me is . . .	
EVERYBODY	Stone Thrower!	
ANANSI	*(Singing a lullaby.)* La, la, la, la, la.	
EVERYBODY	*(Joins in.)* La, la, la, la, la.	40
CUSHION	*(Sings.)* I'm not like the others My sisters and brothers, I don't enjoy shovin' and pushin'.	

 **Esau or Elijah . . . Noah** *Names of people mentioned in the Old Testament.*

I don't have a care
When I rest on a chair,
Which is why they all call me . . .

EVERYBODY   *(Singing.)*
The Cushion.   50

ANANSI   So that's me and my kids,
The children of Anansi.
We get things done,
Though our methods aren't fancy.
But as you'll see
We all have a part,
In the story of adventure

EVERYBODY   Which is just about to start.

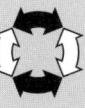 **TALKING AND WRITING:** Rap is a form of music which uses rhyming verses over a strong rhythm. Usually it deals with everyday or topical events. Try writing eight or twelve lines of rap about your school, the area you live in, or something that is in the news at the moment. Then have a go at performing it to your classmates.

SCENE 1

ANANSI's house. ANANSI is collecting a picnic basket, a fishing-rod and a mobile phone to take out. CUSHION is fast asleep. The other CHILDREN are squabbling over the white globe.

ROAD BUILDER	I want it.	1
STONE THROWER	You can't have it.	
SEE DANGER	I'm Dad's favourite child. He wants me to have it.	
GAME SKINNER	No way.	
RIVER DRINKER	Everyone knows he likes me best. Isn't that right, Cushion?	
CUSHION	*(Gives a huge snore.)*	
ROAD BUILDER	Dad!	
ANANSI	What is it now?	
STONE THROWER	This great big ball of light, you found last night.	
ANANSI	What about it?	10
GAME SKINNER	Who do you want to have it?	
ANANSI	I want you all to have it.	
SEE DANGER	But who in particular?	
RIVER DRINKER	You've got to give it to one person. Isn't that right, Cushion?	
CUSHION	*(Sleepily.)* That's right. *(Snores.)*	
ANANSI	Have you never heard of sharing?	
STONE THROWER	We've heard of it.	
RIVER DRINKER	Don't think much of it, though.	

GAME SKINNER	Give it to me. I'm your favourite child.	20
SEE DANGER	No, I am. Who told you to take an umbrella yesterday, because it was going to rain? See Danger did, that's who.	
ROAD BUILDER	Who helped you build a path in the garden? Road Builder did. So I'm your favourite.	
CUSHION	*(Sleepily.)* No! I'm your favourite. Probably. *(Snores.)*	
ANANSI	You want to know the truth? Who I like best and who I like least amongst my children?	
EVERYBODY	Yes.	
ANANSI	I swear by Nyame, the God of All Things, you all drive me equally crazy.	30
EVERYBODY	*(Disappointed.)* Oh.	
ANANSI	And now I've got my fishing rod, picnic and mobile phone, I'm out of here.	
EVERYBODY	But Dad . . .	
ANANSI	*(Raps.)* Instead of staying here, Listening to you dissin' I'm going to the river To enjoy myself fishin'.	
	(ANANSI goes off.)	40
STONE THROWER	Boy, he's angry.	
GAME SKINNER	Always raps when he's mad with us.	
RIVER DRINKER	Dad's right. We shouldn't be arguing all the time.	

 **dissin'** *Slang term for 'showing disrespect'.*

SEE DANGER	I agree, River Drinker.
ROAD BUILDER	Me too.
CUSHION	*(Sleepily.)* Of course we shouldn't. It's obvious Dad wants me to have the globe.
SEE DANGER	No, he wants me to have it!
STONE THROWER	Me!
GAME SKINNER	Me!
ROAD BUILDER	Me!
RIVER DRINKER	Me!

50

Lights down as the CHILDREN argue.

IMPROVISATION: Anansi's children are always disagreeing. Working in pairs, start a conversation where you disagree with everything your partner says. At a given signal from a teacher – a handclap or whistle for example – change your opinion and start agreeing. Start disagreeing again at the next handclap, and so on.

SCENE 2

The river bank. Some steps lead down to the river's edge. ANANSI, carrying a picnic basket, fishing rod and a mobile phone, comes on and goes down the steps.

ANANSI   *(Directly to the audience.)*   1
This is the life.
A little fishing. *(He casts his fishing line.)*
A little boozing. *(He opens the top of the picnic hamper.)*
A little eating
And a little snoozing.

(He settles back comfortably against the riverbank, then sits up suddenly.)

I'd better remember
The kids at home.   10
I'll have a quick word
On my mobile phone.

(He takes out his mobile phone and presses a button. He speaks into the phone.)

Hello . . . Game Skinner . . . I'm just phoning to see you're all behaving yourselves . . . No, I don't like you any better or any worse than your brothers and sisters . . . River Drinker, have you just snatched the phone? . . . No, you can't have the globe. You're meant to share . . . *(The fishing rod twitches in his hand.)* Hold on, I've got a bite. *(He is forced*   20
to stand up.) Wow! This is one big fish! *(He is pulled towards the river.)* Oh no, kids you've got to help me. I'm being pulled into the . . . Hee-elp! *(He is pulled offstage.)*

Lights down on the riverbank.

SCENE 3

ANANSI's house. The white globe lies forgotten in a corner. RIVER DRINKER is holding the mobile phone, while the other CHILDREN crowd round him.

ROAD BUILDER	What's happened to Dad?	1
RIVER DRINKER	The last thing he said . . .	
STONE THROWER	Yes?	
RIVER DRINKER	Was 'glug, glug, glug.'	
SEE DANGER	*(Looking offstage.)* I can see that he's in danger.	
GAME SKINNER	He wouldn't be going 'glug, glug, glug' if he wasn't.	
SEE DANGER	*(Still looking offstage.)* No. I mean I can see where he is and what danger he's in.	
	(All the CHILDREN look in the direction SEE DANGER is looking.)	10
GAME SKINNER	I can't see a thing.	
SEE DANGER	*(Still looking offstage.)* Dad's caught up inside an enormous fish but I can't see how to get to him.	
ROAD BUILDER	I could build a road to him, but I don't know where he is.	
CUSHION	*(Suddenly.)* Listen!	
EVERYBODY	Yes?	
CUSHION	*(Yawns.)*	
RIVER DRINKER	What's the point of listening to a yawn?	
CUSHION	No. Listen to my idea.	
STONE THROWER	We'll try anything once, if it'll save Dad.	20

CUSHION	My idea is . . . *(Stretches and yawns.)*
GAME SKINNER	Are we going to get to this idea before my next birthday?
CUSHION	We've got to work together as a team.
EVERYBODY	A team?
CUSHION	Instead of each doing our own thing, we've got to pull together.
ROAD BUILDER	I don't know.
RIVER DRINKER	We've never done anything like that before. *(RIVER DRINKER's mobile phone rings. STONE THROWER grabs hold of it.)*
STONE THROWER	Is that you, Dad? Is it true you're inside a fish?

30

(A spotlight comes up on the riverbank and steps. ANANSI is curled up at the bottom of them inside a large fish.)

ANANSI	*(Spotlight on ANANSI, rapping into mobile.)* I need help soon, It's a serious matter, Your father's fast becoming A sea-food platter. Get your asses over here And no excuses, Before I dissolve In digestive juices. Help! *(Spotlight down on ANANSI.)*
GAME SKINNER	We've got no choice.
CUSHION	We've got to become a team.
RIVER DRINKER	How do we do that?
CUSHION	See Danger, which way are Dad and the fish?
SEE DANGER	*(Points to ANANSI.)* This way, about half a mile. In a river.
STONE THROWER	We'll never be able to save him.
CUSHION	Let's take it one problem at a time. Road Builder, build us a road in that direction.
ROAD BUILDER	Sure. *(Quietly to CUSHION.)* How am I going to do that? I can't just magic up a JCB.
CUSHION	You're Road Builder, aren't you?
ROAD BUILDER	I certainly am.
CUSHION	Then live up to your name.
ROAD BUILDER	Right. We'll have to make our own machinery.

40

50

JCB *A machine, with a large shovel on the front, used to move rubble and earth. It is named after the initials of its manufacturer, Joseph Cyril Bamford.*

	River Drinker, Game Skinner, Stone Thrower, you make up the engine and the shovel. *(RIVER DRINKER, GAME SKINNER and STONE THROWER make the engine and shovel shape of a JCB.)* See Danger, you're going to show the way.	60
CUSHION	What do I do?	
ROAD BUILDER	You're the cab and I'm the driver. *(CUSHION joins onto the JCB shape. ROAD BUILDER climbs on.)* Let's get this road built! *(With SEE DANGER signalling the way, ROAD BUILDER 'drives' the JCB across the stage to ANANSI.)*	
SEE DANGER	Whoah! Stop right there. *(The JCB dismantles itself.)*	
GAME SKINNER	*(Looking back.)* That's one heck of a road.	
STONE THROWER	Put in four lanes and call it the M25.	70
CUSHION	Quit yapping. We've still got to get Dad out of the river and then out of the fish. *(RIVER DRINKER's mobile phone rings.)*	
RIVER DRINKER	*(Into phone.)* Hello? *(The spotlight comes up on ANANSI again.)*	
ANANSI	*(Rapping into his mobile.)* Don't be slow, Please don't linger, Five more minutes And I'll be a fish finger. Help!	
	(Spotlight down on ANANSI.)	80
CUSHION	River Drinker, you get rid of all the water, so we can get to the fish. Climb up the river bank. *(He points to the top step.)*	
RIVER DRINKER	*(Climbs onto the top step.)* OK. Now what do I do?	

 **M25** *The motorway ring road round London.*

CUSHION	Get down.
RIVER DRINKER	If you say so, Cushion. *(Starts singing and dancing.)* 'Get down and party, That's what you got to do . . .'
CUSHION	No. I mean, get down to the river and drink all the water.
RIVER DRINKER	The whole river?
STONE THROWER	Pretend that it's beer.

90

RIVER DRINKER	You've got it! *(He goes down to the river and mimes drinking all the water, while the others cheer. The spotlight gradually comes up on ANANSI again.)*
SEE DANGER	*(Pointing to ANANSI.)* That's the fish with Dad in!
GAME SKINNER	Brilliant job, River Drinker!
RIVER DRINKER	*(Belches.)* That's it. I'm giving up drinking for good.
GAME SKINNER	But how are we ever going to get Dad out of the fish?
ROAD BUILDER	That's a tough one. We've got a fish, which is like a piece of game.
STONE THROWER	And we've got Dad stuck inside its skin, so what we really need . . .

100

SEE DANGER	Is someone to skin the game.
CUSHION	Any idea who that might be, Game Skinner?
GAME SKINNER	*(Thinks for a moment.)* Nope.
CUSHION	Get moving and cut Dad out. *(GAME SKINNER mimes cutting through the fish that surrounds ANANSI.)*

 **Get down** *To let go and enjoy yourself while dancing.*

STONE THROWER	Well, it looks as though this story is going to have a happy ending.
ROAD BUILDER	It certainly is.
SEE DANGER	*(Looking up into the sky.)* As long as that confused looking sea eagle up in the sky doesn't mistake our dad for a fishy meal.
CUSHION	What eagle?
SEE DANGER	*(Points.)* Up there.
CUSHION	I can't see it. *(RIVER DRINKER and ROAD BUILDER link up to make an eagle.)* Now I do. *(The eagle comes flapping across the stage, as GAME SKINNER manages to pull ANANSI free from the fish.)*
GAME SKINNER	There you are, Dad.
ANANSI	*(Stands up.)* At last I'm freed from the fish's belly. I'm safe and sound.
STONE THROWER	As long as that sea eagle doesn't try and catch you. *(The eagle grabs hold of ANANSI.)*
CUSHION, **GAME SKINNER,** **SEE DANGER** **STONE THROWER**	Uh-oh.
ANANSI	Help! Again!
SEE DANGER	Isn't Dad having a rotten day? *(The eagle drags ANANSI up the steps.)*
ANANSI	*(Raps.)* I wish this hungry eagle Didn't find me appetising 'Cos I hate the sight of heights And we keep on rising. *(CUSHION, GAME SKINNER, SEE DANGER and STONE THROWER slowly crouch down to make ANANSI appear to be rising higher.)*

110

120

130

SEE DANGER	Another minute and Dad'll have disappeared for good.
GAME SKINNER	*(Holding out a stone.)* Take this stone, Stone Thrower!
CUSHION	It's your moment of destiny.
STONE THROWER	*(Getting ready to throw.)* I just hope I don't hit Dad by mistake.
ANANSI	So do I!

140

STONE THROWER	Here goes. *(He takes careful aim, before making a huge throw towards the eagle. There is a drumbeat as the stone hits the eagle.)*
SEE DANGER	Yes!

(The eagle breaks apart. RIVER DRINKER and ROAD BUILDER rejoin the other CHILDREN.)

ANANSI	I'm free! *(He slowly sways down a step.)* But I'm falling towards the hard, hard ground. I need something soft and cuddly to break my fall. *(Everyone else looks at CUSHION.)*
CUSHION	Come on guys . . . I was the brains of this operation . . . Dad weighs a ton.

150

ALL THE OTHER CHILDREN	Cushion!
CUSHION	Oh, all right. *(CUSHION steps forward and catches ANANSI, as ANANSI jumps off the bottom step. Everyone else cheers.)*
ANANSI	Am I really safe, See Danger?
SEE DANGER	*(Looks all around.)* Absolutely.
ANANSI	Then let's go back home and celebrate.
ROAD BUILDER	There's a very good road leads all the way now.

(GAME SKINNER runs ahead, and picks up the globe.)

GAME SKINNER	Now, can I have this, because I cut you out of the fish?

160

STONE THROWER	*(Takes the globe.)* I should have it. I saved you from the eagle.

SEE DANGER	No, I should have it.
ANANSI	Children, haven't you learned anything from this adventure?
CUSHION	Never catch your dad when he falls out of the sky. You hurt your back.
ANANSI	I mean, about the importance of teamwork?
RIVER DRINKER	*(Goes down on one knee. Sentimental.)* I guess, Dad, we all learned the value of working together. *(The other CHILDREN pretend to play violins.)* It isn't enough to think only of yourself. When danger's around, your only hope of escaping it is to pull together as a team.
ANANSI	That's exactly right, River Drinker.
RIVER DRINKER	*(Jumping up and grabbing the globe.)* Do I get to keep this for giving the right answer?
ANANSI	No. *(Takes the globe.)* There's only one place this is going. To Nyame, the God of All Things.
ALL THE CHILDREN	*(Disappointed.)* Awwww.
ANANSI	Nyame can keep it in the Night Sky and there it'll stay, till you kids stop arguing.
GAME SKINNER	That could be forever.
ANANSI	In which case, there'll always be a nice bright light in the sky. Very useful on dark nights.
ROAD BUILDER	Still wish we could keep it.
ANANSI	And every time people see that light, they'll remember the time old Anansi got in trouble with a fish and it needed all his clever children to get him free again.
RIVER DRINKER	Do you really think so?
ANANSI	I know so.

170

180

CUSHION	*(Direct to audience, rapping.)* And that's all we've got to tell you, That's all we've got to say.	190
STONE THROWER	About the great adventure Which came our way.	
RIVER DRINKER	How we all pulled together And rescued Dad.	
GAME SKINNER	From inside the fish, When things were looking bad.	
SEE DANGER	Each and every one of us Needed some skill.	200

ROAD BUILDER   To make sure our father
                   Did not get killed.

ANANSI   And if you want proof
                   You'll see it soon.
                   You know that great white light?

EVERYBODY   Don't you know it's the moon?

DISCUSSION: As a class, discuss the greatest physical danger you, or any of your family, have been in? Was escape possible?

DISCUSSION: Anansi's children all want to be their father's favourite child. What causes most rivalry amongst your family or friends?

IMPROVISATION: Anansi's children link up in the play to make a JCB and an eagle. In small groups, see how many different animals and/or pieces of machinery you can make by joining up. Can you make them move or work?

ARTWORK: Anansi decides he wants to record a rap album, telling of the adventure he's had. Design the cover for the album.

WRITING: Fed up with his children's constant arguing, Anansi contacts a newspaper agony aunt for advice on how to make them get on with each other. Write the letter he sends, and the reply he is given.

Dramascripts

The Casket of Huemac

Dramatised by

ADRIAN FLYNN

WHERE THE TALE COMES FROM

In this play, we see two types of attempted escape – escape from poverty and escape from death. Only one of the attempts is successful.

The play is based on an Aztec story. The Aztecs were a people who lived and ruled in Southern and Central Mexico from the fourteenth to the sixteenth century. Although much of their time was spent in waging war on their neighbours, the Aztecs were also great builders. They created many large pyramid-shaped temples and dedicated them to their gods. One of their most important gods was Huitzilopochtli, the God of War.

To keep their gods happy, the Aztec priests would sacrifice thousands of prisoners of war. In a gruesome ritual, they would tear the living hearts out of the prisoners and offer them up to the gods.

At the start of the play, we find the rag-picker Total looking through the rubbish at Huitzilopochtli's temple. He is desperate to find something valuable so that he and his sister can escape from their dreadful poverty. If they remain poor, there is always a danger the priests will turn on them, when the supply of prisoners runs out.

THE CHARACTERS

TOTAL *a rag-picker.*

URENDEQUA *his sister.*

THE NAUALLI *a magic worker.*

THE FAMILIARS *three (or more) spirits who serve the Naualli.*

THE CASKET OF HUEMAC

SCENE 1

On one side of the stage are some steps leading to the Temple of Huitzilopochtli, the Aztec God of War. TOTAL is searching amongst the rubbish left here. On the other side of the stage is TOTAL's home.

TOTAL	*(To himself.)* Rubbish! Why does nobody throw away anything valuable any more? *(He shakes his head, and carries on searching.)*	1
	(At TOTAL's home, his sister, URENDEQUA, checks her purse, as the NAUALLI, a worker of magic, holds up a small brightly-coloured stone in front of her.)	
URENDEQUA	I don't think we can afford it.	
NAUALLI	It's a very fair price.	
URENDEQUA	I know, but . . .	
NAUALLI	A charm against ill fortune.	10
URENDEQUA	We could do with that. My brother and I are so poor, our whole life is full of bad luck.	

casket *A casket is a small chest for keeping valuable items, such as jewellery in.*

Huemac *A powerful magician in Aztec legend; pronounced 'Way-mac'.*

Huitzilopochtli *Pronounced 'Weet-zeel-o-potch-tly'.*

Naualli *Many Aztecs believed in sorcery and witchcraft, even though the punishment for practising it was death. A naualli was a type of sorcerer.*

NAUALLI	*(Offers her the stone.)* One quill is all it costs.
URENDEQUA	One quill?
	(The NAUALLI nods.)
	That is all we have left. I promised to buy my brother some chocolate with it.
NAUALLI	*(Cups his hands as though they are weighing scales.)* Which is more important? A cup of chocolate? Or protection against harm?
	(TOTAL straightens his back, which is stiff from searching.)

20

 **one quill** *The Aztecs did not have a formal system of money, preferring to barter for the things they wanted. However, valuable items like cocoa beans, or little packets of gold dust – called quills – could be used to make purchases.*

chocolate *Chocolate comes from the Aztec word 'xocolatl'. It was the Aztecs' favourite drink.*

TOTAL	*(To himself.)* How come the other rag-pickers find good stuff from time to time? Old coins, bits of food. I never do. *(He carries on searching.)*
	(The NAUALLI turns the stone in his hands.)
NAUALLI	If your brother were here, I'm sure he'd tell you to buy it.
URENDEQUA	He might do.
NAUALLI	Where is he?
URENDEQUA	At Huitzil's temple.
NAUALLI	Too far to go and ask him. Hold the charm for a moment. *(He gives URENDEQUA the charm.)* Can't you feel the good magic in it? **30**
URENDEQUA	I think so.
NAUALLI	One quill, that's all.
URENDEQUA	If only I knew what Total would think.
	(TOTAL throws down a bundle of rags.)
TOTAL	Absolute rubbish!
	(URENDEQUA takes a packet of gold dust from her purse.)
URENDEQUA	I'm sure he'd want me to buy it. One quill it is.
NAUALLI	You won't regret it. *(He takes the packet from URENDEQUA.)* **40**
	(TOTAL wipes his hands on his clothes.)
TOTAL	I might as well go home. I've earned nothing today. *(Sees a sheet of paper in the rubbish.)* Wait a minute. This could be an important contract someone's thrown away by mistake.

Huitzil's *Short for Huitzilopochtli's.*

I could get a reward for finding it. *(He picks it up and, looks at it.)* Hieroglyphs! I can't read hieroglyphs. It's just more worthless rubbish. *(He starts to crumple it up, then shrugs and tucks it into his shirt.)* You never know. *(He goes offstage.)*

(The NAUALLI starts to leave the hut.)

NAUALLI	Thank you for the money. And if you have any problem with the charm, come to see me.	**50**
URENDEQUA	You live by the lake, don't you?	
NAUALLI	That's right.	
URENDEQUA	I don't know if I should go there.	
NAUALLI	Why not?	
URENDEQUA	Everyone says the lake side is dangerous.	
NAUALLI	Really?	
URENDEQUA	They say all you nauallis who live there use bad magic.	
NAUALLI	Magic isn't bad. In the right hands.	
	(The NAUALLI goes offstage. URENDEQUA looks closely at the charm she has bought. TOTAL comes onstage and joins his sister.)	**60**
TOTAL	Urendequa, I'm home and hungry! *(He slumps onto the floor.)*	
URENDEQUA	*(Hides the charm in a pocket.)* Did you have a good day brother?	
TOTAL	Good? Disastrous, more like.	
URENDEQUA	No scraps of cloth I can mend and sell as clothing?	
TOTAL	No.	

hieroglyphs *The Aztecs didn't use an alphabet. Instead they had a type of picture writing, made up of small drawings which represented objects. These drawing are called hieroglyphs.*

URENDEQUA	No bits of coloured glass I can make into jewellery?	
TOTAL	No! People are too careful about what they throw out these days.	70
URENDEQUA	Are we never going to get away from a life of poverty?	
TOTAL	Only if the priests kill us.	
URENDEQUA	What do you mean, Total?	
TOTAL	The rumour at the temple is, they don't have enough prisoners-of- war.	
URENDEQUA	Enough prisoners for . . .	
TOTAL	The blood sacrifices.	
URENDEQUA	*(Frightened.)* Brother, surely the priests won't want our blood?	80
TOTAL	The gods must have their sacrifice.	
URENDEQUA	But we are just as much Aztecs as the priests themselves.	
TOTAL	A rag-picker and his sister. We're bottom of the pile. No one will miss us if we have our hearts torn out.	
URENDEQUA	*(Takes the charm from her pocket.)* Preserve us.	
TOTAL	What's that?	
URENDEQUA	This? Oh, nothing.	
TOTAL	Urendequa, what is it?	
URENDEQUA	A charm against bad fortune.	
TOTAL	Where did you get it?	90
URENDEQUA	From the naualli who lives by the lake.	

 **the blood sacrifices** *See the introduction to the play.*

TOTAL	That old fraud?
URENDEQUA	He's a good magic worker.
TOTAL	There's no such thing any more.
URENDEQUA	There is!
TOTAL	We haven't had a great magician in this town, since Huemac of the Strong Hand died.
URENDEQUA	This charm really is very good.
TOTAL	Tell me about it, while you prepare my drink of chocolate.
URENDEQUA	Total . . .
TOTAL	It's only the thought of the chocolate which has kept me working all day.
URENDEQUA	There is no chocolate.
TOTAL	What?
URENDEQUA	I spent our last quill on the charm.
TOTAL	What?
URENDEQUA	It will change our luck.
TOTAL	How could you!
URENDEQUA	I was sure you would find something good today.
TOTAL	Well, you were wrong. The only thing I found was this. *(He takes the manuscript from his shirt.)*
URENDEQUA	What is it?
TOTAL	I hoped it might be an important document. I would get a reward for finding it.
URENDEQUA	*(Taking the manuscript from TOTAL.)* Let's see.
TOTAL	But it's utter rubbish. Hieroglyphs I can't read. And now there's no chocolate! *(Puts his head in his hands.)*

100

110

86

URENDEQUA	I can read a little. This looks like the sign for Huemac the Strong Hand.	
TOTAL	You're joking?	120
URENDEQUA	I think it's a message about a box. *(She studies the paper closely.)* Yes, a casket, with all Huemac's treasures in!	
TOTAL	His treasure? *(He looks at the paper.)*	
URENDEQUA	And that sign is for Huitzil's temple. I think the casket is hidden under the steps. You see that drawing?	
TOTAL	*(Looking at the paper.)* Under the fifth . . . No, the sixth step. That's where Huemac's casket is. *(He starts to go off.)* Come on, Urendequa. We're going to be rich.	

TOTAL goes offstage. URENDEQUA follows him.

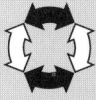

DISCUSSION: Urendequa buys a magic charm, hoping it will protect her and her brother. Some people today think that a rabbit's foot will bring you luck. What other objects can you think of that are meant to be lucky or unlucky?

ARTWORK: Without using any words, draw a message which shows the way to find Huemac's casket.

SCENE 2

The NAUALLI's hut. There are books of spells and magic charms everywhere. The NAUALLI sits on the ground, while his FAMILIARS, dressed in black cloaks and with animal masks, sway and swoop around him, as they bring him dishes of food and drink. Strange, otherworldly music is heard as the FAMILIARS move around. Suddenly, the NAUALLI throws one dish down angrily on the ground.

NAUALLI   Enough!   1

(The FAMILIARS move away from the NAUALLI, hissing with fear.)

I eat and drink until I burst, but I still haven't got what I really want.

(The FAMIILIARS sigh.)

(Angrily the NAUALLI stands up and moves towards the frightened FAMILIARS.) Selling charms, curing warts. These are tricks for children. *(The FAMILIARS sway in a circle around him.)*   10

I want the power to perform strong magic. To be as mighty a magician as . . . *(He stretches out his arms.)* Huemac.

(The FAMILIARS throw themselves to the ground with terror, muttering the name 'HUEMAC.')

(Sadly.) Have no fear. I am no Huemac.

The NAUALLI slowly sits down again, takes a book of spells and starts to read it, while the FAMILIARS take the dishes of food off.

familiars In stories, familiars are supernatural spirits who help sorcerers and witches. They often take the form of animals.

SCENE 3

The steps at Huitzil's temple. TOTAL runs on.

TOTAL	Which step was it?	1
URENDEQUA	*(Comes on with the sheet of paper.)* The sixth.	
TOTAL	Any moment now, we're going to be rich and powerful. Four, five, six. This is the step. *(He tries to lift it.)*	
URENDEQUA	Let me help.	
	(They try to lift the step. It doesn't move. TOTAL sighs and stops work.)	
TOTAL	You must have read the paper wrongly.	
URENDEQUA	I don't think so.	
TOTAL	That's the only explanation. We can't move it.	10
URENDEQUA	Perhaps it's protected by strong magic.	
TOTAL	*(Hits the step.)* It's not fair! The casket's so close. We're so near to escaping from poverty. But how can we fight magic?	
URENDEQUA	We'll get help, Total.	
TOTAL	Help? Who from?	
URENDEQUA	The Naualli who sold me the charm. He's the only magic-worker we know.	
TOTAL	But he'll want to share what we find. Then we'll only have half of Huemac's treasure for ourselves.	
URENDEQUA	Isn't half of something better than all of nothing, brother?	20
	She goes off. After a moment, TOTAL follows her.	

SCENE 4

The NAUALLI's hut. The NAUALLI throws his book of spells down in disgust. The FAMILIARS pull away from him in fright.

NAUALLI	I'm never going to be anything more than a cheap little conjuror. I long to perform some real magic.	1
URENDEQUA	*(Calls from offstage.)* Naualli.	
	(The NAUALLI claps his hands, and his FAMILIARS go off, or disappear by covering themselves with their cloaks.)	
NAUALLI	What is it?	
	(TOTAL and URENDEQUA come onstage.)	
URENDEQUA	Naualli! Can we see you?	
NAUALLI	*(Comes out of his hut.)* What do you want?	
URENDEQUA	Remember me? You sold me a charm.	10
NAUALLI	*(Hurriedly.)* I can't help you if you're not happy with it.	
TOTAL	My sister isn't worried about the charm. She thought you could help us in a much bigger matter.	
NAUALLI	Possibly. If you can afford to pay me.	
URENDEQUA	What would you say to sharing the treasures of Huemac?	
NAUALLI	Huemac of the Strong Hand?	
TOTAL	Do you want to divide up his casket, with all his magic relics?	

 **relics** *Possessions left by someone after they die.*

NAUALLI	You've got it?	
URENDEQUA	We know where it is.	20
NAUALLI	Where?	
TOTAL	If we show you . . .	
URENDEQUA	If you help us recover it . . .	
TOTAL	. . . will you share everything we find, fifty- fifty?	
NAUALLI	Half the treasures of Huemac? Of course.	
URENDEQUA	Then look. *(She unfolds the manuscript.)*	
TOTAL	I found this paper by Huitzil's temple.	
URENDEQUA	I made out the meaning of the signs.	
NAUALLI	This speaks of Huemac.	
URENDEQUA	It says, 'Beneath the sixth step of the temple of Huitzil, lies the casket of Huemac'.	30
NAUALLI	*(Reading excitedly.)* 'Whoever possesses the contents of the casket shall be as great a magician as Huemac himself.'	
TOTAL	My sister and I went to the temple, but when we tried to move the sixth step . . .	
URENDEQUA	It wouldn't budge.	
NAUALLI	Of course not. Huemac won't have made it easy for his casket to be found.	
TOTAL	Will you help us?	
URENDEQUA	If we had even a part of Huemac's power, we could fill our bellies.	40
TOTAL	We'd dress in decent clothes, not the rags I pick from the gutters.	
NAUALLI	Certainly I'll help. Let's get to the temple at once.	

The NAUALLI goes off, followed by TOTAL and URENDEQUA.

SCENE 5

The steps leading up to Huitzil's temple. Fierce drumming and chanting can be heard, as a sacrifice is carried out offstage.

The NAUALLI comes on. He beckons to TOTAL and URENDEQUA who are offstage.

NAUALLI	You're quite safe. That's the last sacrifice of the day.
	(The drumming and chanting stop as TOTAL and URENDEQUA come onstage and go to the steps.)
	(Counting.) . . . three, four, five.
TOTAL	The casket's under the sixth step, but we couldn't move it.
NAUALLI	*(Runs his hands over the step.)* There must be . . .
URENDEQUA	What?
NAUALLI	A hidden spring. Ah, found it. *(He presses the spring.)* Now help me lift this.
TOTAL	It's so heavy.
	(TOTAL and the NAUALLI lift the step off. URENDEQUA lifts a wooden casket out from underneath.)
	Huemac's casket!
URENDEQUA	It's beautiful.
NAUALLI	Satinwood.
TOTAL	Inlaid with silver. I bet inside is full of gold.

1

10

last sacrifice *See the introduction to the play.*

satinwood *Satinwood is a type of tree which gives a hard, glossy wood.*

(*TOTAL seizes the box and takes off the lid.*)

URENDEQUA	What's in it, brother?
TOTAL	(*Disappointed.*) A mirror.
NAUALLI	Let me look. (*He takes the mirror; then says to himself.*) A mirror of life. He who holds it cannot die.
TOTAL	It's just odds and ends.
URENDEQUA	(*Reaching into the box.*) What's this? A rattle?
NAUALLI	(*Takes the rattle, then says to himself.*) Shaken this way, it will banish demons. That way, it will call spirits to you.
URENDEQUA	(*Hurriedly drops what she's found.*) Arrggh! A necklace of fingers!
TOTAL	There are no jewels. No gold dust. (*Taking out a heavy wand.*) I don't know what any of it is for.
URENDEQUA	None of it will fill an empty belly.
NAUALLI	What you have discovered is worthless.
TOTAL	Worthless?
URENDEQUA	So it seems.
NAUALLI	I mean, worthless to ordinary people like you, Total and Urendequa. To someone who knows how to use magic, however . . .
URENDEQUA	It's worth a lot?
NAUALLI	Yes.
TOTAL	Really?
NAUALLI	And I am prepared to give you a good price for your half of the casket.
TOTAL	You want to buy our share?
NAUALLI	Yes.

20

30

40

93

TOTAL	*(Quietly to URENDEQUA.)* Do you think it's a trick?
NAUALLI	You see, I'm being honest with you. I'm letting you know this casket is valuable to me.
URENDEQUA	*(Quietly.)* A mirror, a rattle, none of it is any use to us.
NAUALLI	Name your price.
TOTAL	One moment, Naualli. *(He steps to one side.)* What do you think, Urendequa?

(While TOTAL and URENDEQUA talk, the NAUALLI lovingly handles the objects from Huemac's casket.)

URENDEQUA	I think we should sell everything.
TOTAL	How much for?
URENDEQUA	Fifty quills would stop us being hungry for a year.
TOTAL	If he pays a hundred quills, we could buy ourselves somewhere decent to live.
URENDEQUA	He'll never pay a hundred.
TOTAL	Look at him. He's in love with the casket.
URENDEQUA	Go on. Ask for a hundred then.
TOTAL	Or maybe even two hundred.
URENDEQUA	Two hundred!
TOTAL	With two hundred quills, I need never work again.
URENDEQUA	It's too much.
TOTAL	And we could live in the nicest part of the city.
URENDEQUA	Do you really think so?
TOTAL	No one would look down on me as a rag-picker any more.
URENDEQUA	The priests wouldn't dare think of us for the blood sacrifices.

50

60

TOTAL	Exactly.	70
URENDEQUA	Go on. Ask for two hundred quills.	
TOTAL	*(Turns back to the NAUALLI.)* Naualli, we have decided to sell.	
NAUALLI	Good.	
TOTAL	But only for two hundred . . . no, three hundred quills.	
URENDEQUA	*(Surprised.)* Three hundred?	
TOTAL	*(Quietly to URENDEQUA.)* Always start by asking for more than you want.	
NAUALLI	Very well. Three hundred quills it is.	
TOTAL	*(Astonished.)* You agree?	
NAUALLI	The casket is too important to haggle over. *(He takes three bags of gold dust from his belt.)* There you are.	80
URENDEQUA	Total! Life's going to be marvellous. No more cold nights. No more sleeping with the rats. No more lying awake because our bellies cry out that they're empty.	
TOTAL	*(Quietly.)* I'm not sure.	
URENDEQUA	What's wrong?	
TOTAL	*(Quietly.)* Did you see how quickly he agreed?	
URENDEQUA	Yes, and I'm so happy. Thank you, Naualli.	
	(TOTAL takes URENDEQUA aside, while the NAUALLI explores the casket further.)	90
TOTAL	*(Quietly.)* Don't you understand? If he agreed so readily to three hundred, the casket must be worth much more. He's tricked us.	

haggle *To argue over the price of something.*

URENDEQUA	What does it matter if he has?
TOTAL	We could get more gold.
URENDEQUA	But we're free from poverty now.
TOTAL	Not rich though. Not really rich.
URENDEQUA	*(Worried.)* Total . . .
	(TOTAL goes back to the casket and picks up the wand.)
TOTAL	That three hundred quills?
NAUALLI	Yes?
TOTAL	You realise that was for the casket itself? Not for the contents.
NAUALLI	Three hundred quills was for everything.
TOTAL	No. If you wanted this wand for example, you must pay extra.
NAUALLI	Be careful with that. It is a wand of power.
URENDEQUA	We've got all we need. Let's go home, Total.
TOTAL	This wand has got to be worth another hundred quills at least.
NAUALLI	You're getting no more gold dust.
TOTAL	In fact, I want another hundred and fifty quills for it.
NAUALLI	No.
TOTAL	I insist.
NAUALLI	Give that to me.
TOTAL	You want it? OK. *(He strikes NAUALLI with the wand.)*
URENDEQUA	Total! Stop!
	(The NAUALLI sinks slowly to the ground.)
TOTAL	The wand is powerful. It only needed one blow.

100

110

URENDEQUA	You've killed him.	120
TOTAL	Looks like it, doesn't it?	
URENDEQUA	Why?	
TOTAL	Don't you understand? Three hundred quills is nothing. The Naualli must have been planning to use this stuff of Huemac's to magic up thousands of quills. That's what I'll do. We'll be the richest people in the city.	
URENDEQUA	To kill the Naualli was wrong.	
TOTAL	Only if we're caught. Quick, help me wrap him in his cloak. *(URENDEQUA doesn't move.)* Come on. We'll drag his body to the lake, where no one will find him.	130
URENDEQUA	I'm afraid.	
TOTAL	Then carry the casket and I'll drag the body. As soon as he's thrown in the water, we can start our new life.	

TOTAL drags the NAUALLI off. URENDEQUA picks up the casket and its contents and follows her brother off.

 **HOT-SEATING:** Think about the moment when Huemac's casket is opened, and what it means to Total and the Naualli. In small groups, hot-seat both of them in turn. Ask what their feelings are, how it will affect their plans for the future, and so on.

IMPROVISATION: Imagine an Aztec priest has heard about the Naualli's disappearance and is conducting interviews with anyone who might know about it. Act out what happens when Urendequa and Total are interviewed.

SCENE 6

The NAUALLI's hut. The FAMILIARS are moving slowly around it. Otherworldly music is heard.

1ST FAMILIAR	Where is he?	1
2ND FAMILIAR	Where is our master?	
3RD FAMILIAR	Gone.	
ALL THREE FAMILIARS	Gone!	
1ST FAMILIAR	Who has caused this?	
2ND FAMILIAR	Who's responsible?	
3RD FAMILIAR	Who shall pay?	
ALL THREE FAMILIARS	Someone shall pay!	

(TOTAL, now wearing the NAUALLI's cloak, comes on carrying Huemac's casket. URENDEQUA follows him reluctantly.) 10

URENDEQUA   Please, Total, you shouldn't come to this hut.

(The FAMILIARS cover their faces and hide themselves in the hut.)

TOTAL   Why not?

URENDEQUA   You know why not. You murdered the Naualli who lived here.

TOTAL   And since he won't need it any more, I've come to take his place. *(He steps up to the door of the hut.)* Aren't you coming in too?

URENDEQUA   No!

TOTAL   There's no sense such a good hut being wasted. Besides,   20

	I don't know how to make all this magic stuff work.
URENDEQUA	I wish we'd never found out about Huemac's casket.
TOTAL	The Naualli is bound to have had some books of spells. I shall spend the night here, learning how to be a magician.
URENDEQUA	You'll stay all night?
TOTAL	Of course. By the morning I will know exactly how to use the casket.
URENDEQUA	Brother, it's too dangerous to stay.
TOTAL	Nonsense.
URENDEQUA	The dead man's spirit will haunt you.
TOTAL	You don't know what you're talking about.
URENDEQUA	Even when we threw his body in the water, his eyes never closed.
TOTAL	What does that matter?
URENDEQUA	It was as though he wasn't dead.
TOTAL	(*Laughs.*) Dead enough.
URENDEQUA	We should have been happy with the three hundred quills.
TOTAL	Go away if you're scared. Come back in the morning.
URENDEQUA	Total, come home with me.
TOTAL	Go! By the time you see me tomorrow, I'll know how to make us three thousand quills, not three hundred.

30

40

(*URENDEQUA goes off, while TOTAL enters the hut. He looks around.*)

Now where did that old Naualli keep his spells?

(*The 1st FAMILIAR produces a book and slides it across the floor in front of TOTAL.*)

That's what I need.

99

(As TOTAL bends to pick it up, the 2nd FAMILIAR snatches it up and slowly waves it in front of TOTAL. TOTAL tries to grab it, but the 2nd FAMILIAR passes it to the 3rd.)   **50**

2ND FAMILIAR   He sees, but he does not see.

TOTAL   *(Nervous.)* A voice? Is someone there?

3RD FAMILIAR   He hears, but he does not hear.

TOTAL   I'm not frightened!

(The FAMILIARS pass the book round between them.)

I'm not the least bit frightened. *(1st FAMILIAR lets TOTAL take the book.)*

A little magic doesn't scare me. I mean to be a magician myself. I mean to be as powerful as Huemac.

FAMILIARS   *(Moving and chanting.)* Huemac, Huemac, Huemac, Huemac!   **60**

TOTAL   *(Trying to stay calm.)* It's my imagination, that's all. I'll soon have learned enough to protect myself from any harm. *(He opens the book and starts to read.)*

(The FAMILIARS start moving round TOTAL. Soft, otherworldly music is heard once more.)

1ST FAMILIAR   He wants to be like Huemac.

2ND FAMILIAR   He wants to be a great magician.

3RD FAMILIAR   But he's only a murderer.

FAMILIARS   *(Chanting.)* Murderer, murderer, murderer!

TOTAL   There's no one there. I know there isn't.   **70**

FAMILIARS   Murderer!

TOTAL   It's just the sound of bats and mice scurrying. Nothing to be afraid of.

scurrying *Moving quickly.*

(The 2nd FAMILIAR brushes a bony hand against TOTAL's cheek. TOTAL screams.)

FAMILIARS   Murderer, murderer, murderer!

TOTAL   *(Looks into the book of spells and reads.)* 'Using a rattle to banish spirits.' That's the spell I need. There's a rattle in the casket. I'll get rid of these voices. *(He snatches the rattle from the casket, then checks in the book.)* Shaking the rattle one way sends the spirits away. But if you shake it the other, you call them to you. What if I do it wrongly?

80

FAMILIARS   He wants to be like Huemac, but he's scared to death.

1ST FAMILIAR	To death.
2ND FAMILIAR	To death.
3RD FAMILIAR	To death.
TOTAL	I must do something to stop these dreadful voices. *(He starts shaking the rattle. The FAMILIARS stop moving and become silent.)* That's it. It must be working. I can't hear anything, any more. *(He shakes the rattle again.)* 90
1ST FAMILIAR	Why does he call us?
2ND FAMILIAR	He must want us.
3RD FAMILIAR	Let's go to him.
ALL THREE FAMILIARS	*(Chanting.)* Let's go to him, let's go to him.

They continue chanting as they circle TOTAL, drawing ever closer to him. TOTAL slowly sinks to the ground in terror as the FAMILIARS surround him. Blackout.

 **MIME/MOVEMENT:** Act out Total's haunted night in the hut, using music and mime to create a creepy atmosphere. If you have the equipment to do this as black light theatre, even better. The book of spells and other objects should appear to move round as though by magic!

SCENE 7

The NAUALLI's hut, the next morning. The FAMILIARS have gone. A cloak is lying in the middle of the floor, with a body under it. Next to it are the book of spells and Huemac's casket.

URENDEQUA comes on, carrying a piece of bread and a beaker of water.

URENDEQUA	Total! Total, I've brought you breakfast. Come out of the hut . . . Total? Are you all right? *(Nervously, she looks inside the hut. She sees the cloak.)* Total, wake up! Come outside and have breakfast . . . He must be fast asleep, not to hear me. I suppose I'd better go in.	1
	(She puts down the bread and water, then goes into the hut. She lifts the cloak from the floor, revealing the NAUALLI underneath. URENDEQUA screams.)	
NAUALLI	What's the matter? Have I got such a frightening face?	
URENDEQUA	But you were . . . you were . . .	10
NAUALLI	Dead?	
URENDEQUA	Yes! We threw you in the lake.	
NAUALLI	It takes a great deal to kill a naualli. Especially one who holds Huemac's mirror of life. *(The NAUALLI shows he has the mirror in his hand.)*	
URENDEQUA	Where's my brother?	
NAUALLI	Not here.	
URENDEQUA	I must look for him.	
NAUALLI	Urendequa, you won't find him any more. Not in this world.	20

URENDEQUA   What do you mean?

NAUALLI   He has escaped from poverty once and for all.

URENDEQUA   Where is he?

NAUALLI   In a place it is better not even to dream of.

URENDEQUA   Poor Total. I must help him.

NAUALLI   He has gone beyond all help. He is dead.

URENDEQUA   *(Horrified, she takes three bags of gold dust from her pockets and holds them out to the NAUALLI.)* Here.

NAUALLI   The quills are yours, whatever your brother has done.

URENDEQUA   I don't want them. *(She drops the bags on the ground, then takes out the charm and throws it on the ground also.)* Nor your charm!   30

NAUALLI   These are your things. I have my casket, you must take your gold.

URENDEQUA   Never.

NAUALLI   *(Picks up and offers her one of the bags.)* With this, you will be free of your poverty, free of your hunger.

URENDEQUA   There are worse things than hunger. Much worse things. *(She howls with despair.)* Aiieee! I curse the day I ever heard of Huemac.   40

                URENDEQUA slowly sinks to her knees and cries.

                Otherworldly music, as the NAUALLI looks at her for a moment, then shakes his head, picks up the casket and goes off.

                Blackout.

DISCUSSION: The Naualli manages to escape death, but Total fails to escape from poverty, dying in the attempt to do so. However, at one point in the play, when he is offered three hundred quills for Huemac's casket, Total did have the opportunity to free himself from poverty for good. Why do you think he didn't take it? What other ways might Total and Urendequa have tried to escape from poverty?

ARTWORK: Draw or make Huemac's casket. What patterns and signs would be on it?

RESEARCH: Find out as much as you can about the Aztecs. What gods, other than Huitzilopochtli, did they believe in? What crafts were they most skilful at? How was the Aztec nation finally conquered?

WRITING: Imagine Urendequa keeps a diary. Write the entry on the day her brother dies, explaining how she feels about everything that has happened, and what she intends to do in the future now he's gone.

LOOKING BACK AT THE PLAYS

1 DISCUSSION

The four plays deal with different types of escape. As a class, brainstorm as many different situations people might want to escape from as you can think of. Then think of the methods they might use to escape from those situations.

2 DISCUSSION

In pairs, discuss which of the plays you like best, and which you like least. List them in order, from favourite to least favourite, giving reasons for your decisions. Then compare your list with another pair.

3 PERFORMANCE

In groups, choose a scene from two different plays. Make sure they are quite different in tone – one could be comic, one could be sad, for example. Practise and perform the two scenes, trying to bring out the differences between them as much as possible.

4 MIME/DANCE

Choose the story of one of the plays to perform in mime or dance. Select music which helps create the appropriate atmosphere and, if possible, use costume or masks to help an audience understand who the characters are and what they are doing.

5 WRITING

Imagine you are trapped in a situation you are determined to escape from. Write a secret diary while you plan and prepare your escape attempt. Make it clear why you are so desperate to get away and what the consequences will be if your attempt fails.

6 ARTWORK

Imagine you are putting on a performance of these four plays. Design and make a poster for it, using one strong, central image to suggest the idea of 'escape'.